THE KAYAK SHOP

THE KAYAK SHOP

Three Elegant Wooden Kayaks Anyone Can Build

Chris Kulczycki

Ragged Mountain Press
Camden, Maine

International Marine/
Ragged Mountain Press

A Division of The McGraw-Hill Companies

10 9 8

Library of Congress Cataloging-in-Publication Data

Kulczycki, Chris, 1958–
    The kayak shop : three elegant wooden kayaks anyone can build / Chris Kulczycki.
    p.   cm.
    Includes index.
    ISBN 0-07-035519-3 (acid-free paper)
    1. Kayaks—Design and construction—Amateurs's manuals. I. Title.
VM353.K85   1993
623.8'29—dc20   93–23886
                                      CIP

Questions regarding the content of this book should be addressed to:
Ragged Mountain Press
P.O. Box 220
Camden, ME 04843

Questions regarding the ordering of this book should be addressed to:
The McGraw-Hill Companies
Customer Service Department
P.O. Box 547
Blacklick, OH 43004
Retail Customers: 1-800-262-4729
Bookstores: 1-800-722-4726

A portion of the profits from the sale of each Ragged Mountain Press book is donated to an environmental cause.

This book is printed on 60-pound Renew Opaque Vellum, an acid-free paper which contains 50 percent recycled waste paper (preconsumer) and 10 percent postconsumer waste paper.

Printed by R. R. Donnelley, Crawfordsville, IN
Design by Silverline Studio, Camden, Maine
Production by Janet Robbins
Edited by Jim Babb, Michael S. Crowley, and Pamela Benner

For Annette

"For she is such a smart little craft,
Such a neat little, sweet little craft–
Such a bright little,
Tight little,
Slight little,
Light little,
Trim little, slim little craft."
                    —W. S. Gilbert, *Ruddigore II*

Contents

Acknowledgments

I cannot imagine a book that's the work of only the author. Many people helped make *The Kayak Shop* possible. My wife, Annette, put up with sawdust and wood shavings in our rugs, wet paddle jackets in our kitchen, reams of plans in our living room, drafting projects on the dining table, manuscript pages everywhere, and me. She edited and proofread, helped with the photography, and even lent a hand in the shop. Bob Grove, photographer, boatbuilder, and, most recently, boat designer, printed most of the photos in this book, built and tested my designs, and contributed many ideas incorporated in them. Clay Corry also proofread, helped with photos, and paddled my designs.

I am also indebted to the many boatbuilders who have bought my plans, built my designs, and offered their insights and ideas, and to several "rival" boatbuilders and kayak designers who offered their ideas, photos, and specifications for use in this volume. Parts of *The Kayak Shop* are adapted from articles I wrote for *Sea Kayaker* and *Fine Woodworking* magazines, and from manuals written for Chesapeake Light Craft kits and plans.

Introduction

The double-paddle canoe gives the most fun for the money of any type of boat a person can possess.
—L. Francis Herreshoff, *Sensible Cruising Designs*

I first paddled a kayak when I was ten years old. My family spent a vacation paddling old wooden doubles on the lakes of western Poland. Those weeks launched my love of boats, particularly of kayaks. Not long after, I built my first boat: a boxlike, 6-foot pram nailed together from paneling and 2 x 4s that I'd found in our garage. My parents returned home one day to find the patio transformed into a boatyard. Not appreciative of my breakthroughs in naval architecture, they forbade me to launch my first design. But, convinced my craft was as seaworthy as the *Queen Mary*, I recruited a friend to help me carry it to a nearby stream for sea trials. We didn't have any oars or paddles, but that didn't matter much since our stream was only 20 feet wide and, fortunately, flowed slowly. In any case my pram leaked too much to go far.

Though my sporting interests soon turned to rock climbing and later sailing, memories of kayaks and home-built boats never faded. But not until 20 years after paddling that first kayak did I decide to build my own. I'd built a few dinghies in those 20 years, and I'd even worked as a marine carpenter for a summer, so I had confidence that my kayak would come out nicely. Still I was surprised at how well that first kayak did come out. It wasn't that I was a master boatbuilder—I'll never be accused of that—but rather that plywood kayaks are easy to build. In fact, you can probably build as nice a kayak as you can buy.

Building boats has long been known to be of therapeutic value, perhaps of only slightly less therapeutic value than paddling them. I came upon this bit of truth while working in a rather stressful managerial position. I would return home after work, tired, anxious, tense, and hating the world, go into my shop and in a few hours emerge refreshed and relaxed. It took a year of doing this to convince me that there was a better way to spend my days; some of us are slow learners.

This slim volume will endeavor to explain how to build three types of kayaks. Armed with this knowledge, a few simple tools, and a bit of good wood, you'll be ready to build a 25-pound kayak to paddle around your farm pond, or an 18-foot sea kayak to take you on expeditions to remote regions.

Chapter 1
The Wooden Kayak

This book will guide you through building a round-bottomed, high-performance 16-foot single-seat kayak; a hard-chine 18-foot sea kayak; and a compounded-plywood 20-foot double. Plans for each of these three boats are reproduced and discussed in Chapter 5. But the same methods used to build these kayaks can be applied to building many other kayaks drawn by other designers or by you.

I'll assume that you have just an elementary knowledge of woodworking; those of you who are expert boatbuilders or cabinetmakers will have to bear with us. And I'll also assume that you know a little about kayaks—that is, that you've paddled a few.

The themes here are simplicity, light weight, economy, and aesthetics. While some designs require that you construct large jigs and strongbacks to build the kayak on, the designs discussed here don't, nor do they rely on extensive frameworks. You won't need to buy any unusual tools, and the materials you'll use, while not available everywhere, can certainly be ordered and shipped anywhere. These kayaks are at least a third lighter than most plastic kayaks, yet they are rigid and strong. They can be built for a half or even a quarter the

This hard-chine sea kayak, the Patuxent, is one of my latest designs. It's lighter, faster, and just as durable as comparable fiberglass kayaks, yet it can be built in two weeks and for half the cost of the 'glass boat.

The Pocomoke and the Yare, two designs featured in this book, are good examples of the complex shapes possible with compounded-plywood designs. The Pocomoke is 19 feet, 10 inches long and weighs 52 pounds; the 16-foot 3-inch Yare weighs 26 pounds.

cost of a comparable fiberglass kayak, but they often perform better. And they are, at least to my eye, quite handsome.

Why Wood?

A tree must bend and flex thousands of times each windy day, millions of times in a year, yet it still returns to its original shape. Its branches must be strong and light, yet stiff enough to hold their load of leaves. Protected by its coating of bark, it must resist the assaults of sun, water, and wind. These same characteristics—light weight, strength, resistance to fatigue, and durability—make wood an excellent material for the construction of your kayak.

Though wood has lower initial strength than some other materials used in boatbuilding, its other properties make up for this. Consider that even with the arrival of such exotic materials as carbon fiber, Nomex, and Kevlar, some of today's fastest multihull sailboats are built of wood and epoxy. There are few craft that experience the loads and the stresses of an ocean-racing multihull and that pay so high a price in performance for extra weight.

Beyond weight and strength, stiffness and resistance to fatigue must be considered when selecting the material for a kayak. Studies have shown wood to be up to 10 times stiffer than fiberglass by weight, and nearly 6 times stiffer than Kevlar/epoxy composite. Though these studies aren't directly applicable to kayak construction, they do illustrate that wood is a very stiff material and a stiff boat tends to be faster, particularly in calm water, since energy is not wasted in flexing the hull.

Plywood kayaks are light. That's me holding up my 26-pound Yare. This is the way I usually carry it to the water. (Photo by Annette Najjar)

A kayak must have more than just initial strength; its strength must be retained despite repeated cycles of tension and compression from rough seas and spirited paddling. Wood loses very little strength even after millions of cycles of loading and unloading. That tree, flexing millions of times a year, may live for hundreds or even thousands of years if man or natural disaster doesn't intervene. This resistance to fatigue gives wood an advantage over many materials when a long-lasting and reliable hull is the objective.

Toughness or resistance to tearing, puncturing, and abrasion is an important consideration, particularly if a kayak is launched from and landed on rocky shores. Fiberglass and polyethylene have some advantage over wood in this quality, but by sheathing the wooden hull with a thin layer of fiberglass cloth, Kevlar, or Dynel its toughness can be greatly improved.

Woods's traditional drawbacks have largely been solved by modern technology. The problem of rot has been greatly reduced, though not totally eliminated, by modern epoxy saturation methods. The problem of finding suitable wood has been solved by the advent of truly high-quality plywoods. And the problem of waterproof glue has been eliminated by modern epoxy systems. Modern methods of wooden-boat building bear little resemblance to those of 50 years ago. Wood has become a high-tech material.

However much we appreciate the engineering properties of wood, it is wood's aesthetic qualities that are most remarkable. No other material inspires such a bond between the paddler and the kayak. People seem drawn to wooden boats, perhaps as a reaction to the profusion of artificial materials that surround us. Wooden kayaks feel better and paddle better than do fiberglass boats. I don't know why this is; perhaps I only imagine it—but a lot of other folks imagine it,

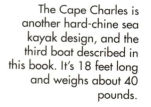

The Cape Charles is another hard-chine sea kayak design, and the third boat described in this book. It's 18 feet long and weighs about 40 pounds.

Dennis Davis was among the first to design and build compounded-plywood kayaks. This DK-13 is one of his many popular designs. It's also the first compounded-plywood boat that I built.

too. Many sailors have written that they feel their wooden boats are alive, and that they miss that feeling when they sail a fiberglass boat. Well, I wouldn't go that far, but I'll admit that wooden kayaks are somehow more satisfying to paddle. Perhaps this impression can be compared to that of the angler who insists on using a split Tonkin bamboo rod for fly fishing, even though perfectly good graphite rods are available at a quarter of their cost.

So why aren't more kayaks built of wood? Well more and more are. In fact there's been a tremendous revival of wooden-boat building in general. But wood isn't so well suited to production building as are plastics, so mainstream builders aren't likely to use it. Still, there are many skilled wooden-boat builders who build kayaks for a small number of clients.

Fortunately, wood is readily available, relatively inexpensive, and can be worked with a minimum of tools and skills. And wood is a satisfying material to work with; the texture, appearance, and even smell of it is pleasing. Most of us regard 40 or 60 hours of cutting, sanding, planing, and varnishing a thoroughly agreeable way to spend some free time. The labor-intensive process the production builder wants to avoid is recreation to the amateur.

Building with Plywood

When plywood kayaks are mentioned, some paddlers recoil at the thought of slab-sided monstrosities built from plans published in a

The Sparrowhawk is one of the spirited and pretty sailing kayaks designed and built by Daniel Leonard of Wind Horse Marine. (Photo courtesy Wind Horse Marine)

Okay, it's not really a kayak, but Bob Grove's double-paddle piroque is an example of the many other types of craft that can be built using some of the same techniques we'll discuss. Plans are available from Chesapeake Light Craft. (Photo by Bob Grove)

1935 issue of *Home Woodbutcher*. Well, plywood kayaks have come a long way since those days. Flip through this book; I think you'll agree that plywood kayaks can be quite graceful.

Most plywood kayaks are of *hard-chine* design. That is, their hulls are composed of relatively flat panels that are joined at angles to form the hull. Though some paddlers may scoff at hard-chine designs, they have several advantages over round-bottomed boats: they are well suited to heavy loads; they have high initial stability, which is nice on long trips; and the chines help in "carving" turns. Additionally, they are very straightforward to build.

For ultimate speed and efficiency, however, nothing moves like a round-bottomed boat. Most round-bottomed plywood kayaks are built using a technique variously called compounded plywood, bent plywood, stressed plywood, developed plywood, and, most descriptively, tortured plywood. This method was pioneered in the early 1960s by catamaran builders and by kayak designer Dennis Davis. *Compounded-plywood* construction involves bending thin plywood in two planes simultaneously, producing a compound curve. It might be thought of as a modern version of the method used to build birch bark canoes. Compounded-plywood boats can have very pleasing rounded forms that some have described as "organic."

Modern plywood kayaks, whether hard-chine or round-bottomed, rarely need frames. This contributes to their light weight and the simplicity of their construction. They are *monocoque* structures, meaning they rely primarily on their skins, rather than on internal members, for strength. Many plywood kayaks, including all of my designs, can be constructed without forms or jigs. Today's plywoods bend so easily and consistently that special bending methods like steaming or soaking the wood aren't necessary.

The durability of modern wooden boats is due largely to the use of epoxy. Epoxy resin is a rather thin liquid that when mixed with a

These Sea Tamer sea kayaks can be built in two or three sections so they can be taken apart and stored in the closet. South Shore Boatworks will also sell you plans or a kit for a one-piece version, but you'll need a bigger closet. They also build a double. (Photo courtesy South Shore Boatworks)

hardener becomes a tenacious adhesive that solidifies into a hard clear plastic. Brushed onto the wood's surface, epoxy penetrates into the wood fibers, forming a tough skin and preventing the passage of water and fungus that can cause wood to rot.

The Skills You'll Need

You don't need to be an expert woodworker to build a plywood kayak. In fact, most of the skills you'll need can be learned in a few hours. You must know how to use a sabersaw, a block plane, a drill, and a few other basic tools. You must be able to measure and use a carpenter's square. Perhaps the hardest skill to learn is the patience to slow down every once in a while, stand back, and make sure everything is going as you intend.

If you have no woodworking experience, limited time, or want to improve your skills quickly, consider attending a kayak building or boatbuilding class or seminar. There are several boatbuilding schools in the country that teach week-long courses in kayak building; in most, you'll actually build your own boat during the course. Wouldn't that be a nice way to spend a vacation?

Also, look into local boatbuilding clubs. There's a strong network of woodworkers and wooden-boat builders in many parts of the country. I belong to a traditional small-boat association whose membership includes three professional wooden-boat builders and two naval architects who are usually willing to dispense free advice to fellow members. In addition, our club holds demonstrations of building techniques, on-the-water rallies, and talks by both amateur and

This is an early version of the Skua 16 that I designed for *Sea Kayaker* magazine; this design eventually evolved into the Yare.

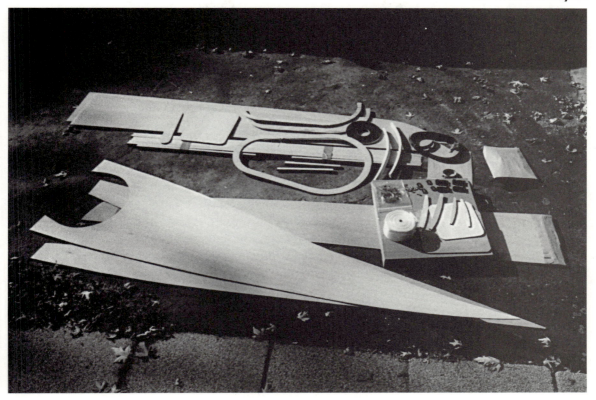

professional boatbuilders. I can even borrow a tool I need from some of the other members.

The hardest part of building your own kayak is getting started. By opening this book you've done that. But before you take saw to wood, read the entire book. Knowing what comes next can save you substantial time and trouble when you're building.

If you don't have much time, you can buy a kayak kit. This Chesapeake Light Craft kit becomes a Yare.

Chapter 2
The Design

Kayaks are among the simplest of boats, yet thousands of kayak designs have been created, each of them someone's idea of the perfect boat. Your first step in building a kayak is choosing a design or drawing your own. If you're an experienced kayaker, you'll probably have an idea of how a boat will paddle just from looking at it. If you're not experienced, take every opportunity to paddle different boats before selecting one to build. In either case, knowing a little about how kayak, paddler, and water interact and about the elements of a kayak's design will help you make a wise choice.

Kayak design is not a science; it's a blend of art, intuition, and engineering. This becomes obvious to me every time I launch a new design. Whether I've drawn the boat or built it to someone else's design, I am always surprised by some aspect of the kayak's performance. Still, using a blend of experience and theory, you'll have a pretty good shot at choosing the boat that's right for you.

Length

Length is usually the first dimension you'll look at. To a large degree, a kayak's length determines how fast it can go, how stable it is, and

Paddle as many boats as you can and see how far you can push them. Clay Corry tries out my prototype Skua 16.

how much it will hold. There are really two separate lengths that must be considered for every boat. The first is the length overall, or *LOA*: this is the distance between the outside faces of the bow and stern. The length on the waterline, or *LWL*, is the more important length measurement: the LWL is the distance between the *immersed* ends of the kayak when it's normally loaded.

Most benefits of length are due to a long LWL, and not to a long LOA. A boat with a LOA much longer than its LWL is said to have long overhangs. Long overhanging bows and sterns are often added to a design for cosmetic reasons. Some paddlers feel that long overhanging bows are beneficial in rough waters. But similar advantages can be achieved with a moderate overhang by increasing the volume in the bow. Long overhangs, particularly if they are upswept as in some "Greenland-style" kayaks, add considerable lateral surface area that makes a boat more difficult to handle in strong winds.

Most paddlers know that a boat's top speed is related to its length. A boat creates a bow wave where it cuts through the water and a stern wave as the water comes together again at the boat's end; in order for waves to move faster they must be farther apart. So a long boat, with its bow and stern waves farther apart, will be able to go faster. A boat's theoretical top speed, or *hull speed*, in knots (a knot is 1.15 m.p.h.) is 1.34 times the square root of the LWL. Now before you write to ask me why Uncle Fred's 17-foot speedboat can go 50 knots while your 17-foot sea kayak will only go 5 knots, let me explain that this rule doesn't apply to high-powered planing boats, which slide over the water, not through it. Actually, your kayak can also attain very high speeds when surfing down waves. Even on flat water, a kayak, like many boats with very narrow hulls, is capable of speeds slightly higher than its theoretical hull speed.

The importance of length as related to speed can be overemphasized. A paddler can generate about one-quarter horsepower, so the limiting factor in speed is the drag that your paddling must overcome and not theoretical hull speed. Once the kayak's LWL approaches 17 feet or so, little or no speed will be gained by lengthening it. You'll rarely paddle fast enough to achieve hull speed in a kayak. At average touring speeds, however, a boat with a longer LWL will be easier to paddle, assuming everything else is equal.

There's more to be gained from length than just speed. If you compare two kayaks of different lengths but otherwise similar design, you'll find that the longer boat has several advantages over the shorter one. The longer boat won't pitch as violently in steep waves, and it will be more stable. It will have a higher volume and will hold more gear. And the longer boat will track, or go in a straight line, better than the shorter kayak.

On the other hand, there are some disadvantages to longer kayaks. Comparing the same two boats, you'll notice that the longer one is less maneuverable, requires more materials to build, and is heavier and more expensive. Finally, a long boat will be harder to store and transport. Single sea kayaks with a LWL of 14 feet to 18 feet seem ideal. Doubles appear to work best with a LWL of 17 feet to 20 feet. Flat-water kayaks, very wide kayaks, and kayaks intended for lighter loads may be shorter. High-performance kayaks and racing kayaks, if not limited by rules, may be longer.

Beam and Cross Section

After length, you'll look at a kayak's beam, or width. Beam, like length, affects a kayak's volume, stability, and speed. You must consider the beam both at the waterline and overall. Closely related to beam is the cross-sectional shape of the kayak's hull. It may be round-bottomed, flat-bottomed, V-bottomed, or, more commonly, a combination of these shapes.

It's generally thought that wider boats are more stable. This is often, though not always, true. Stability has two elements: initial and ultimate. *Initial stability* is seen in a skiff or a beamy, flat-bottomed kayak. A boat with high initial stability doesn't feel tippy, or tender, but if it's heeled over too far it capsizes without warning. A boat with high *ultimate stability*, such as a kayak with a rounded bottom and flared sides, may be tender at first but as it heels, more of the hull is immersed, increasing resistance to capsize. Initial heeling actually helps skilled paddlers control the boat by enabling them to easily lean into a turn and into waves when in rough seas. Round-bottomed and V-bottomed boats and craft with very narrow waterline beams usually have lower initial stability. Boats with flared sides and high volume tend to have high ultimate stability.

A good way to improve stability is not by increasing the beam but by lowering the boat's center of gravity. Moving a kayak's seat down an inch or two can result in a dramatic increase in stability. All the weight in a kayak should be placed as low as possible, including your seat.

Shorter kayaks must be wider so they are able to hold their intended cargos. But there are several disadvantages to beamy kayaks. They are usually slower than narrower boats and often don't track as well. In addition, a normal-length paddle may strike the gunnels of a wide kayak, and beamy kayaks can be unattractive. For single-seat kayaks, a beam of 19 inches to 26 inches is reasonable while doubles may be as wide as 32 inches.

Prismatic Coefficient and Hull Form

Another measurement related to a boat's beam and cross section is its *prismatic coefficient*, or Cp. A kayak's Cp describes how full or fine ended the hull is. A boat with a high Cp has its volume distributed along its length, causing the ends to have a "full" shape. A boat with a low Cp has its volume concentrated near the center, and its ends are finely tapered. Cp is the ratio between the volume of displacement (how much water a loaded boat displaces) and the volume of a prism that has the same length as the LWL and the same cross-sectional area as the widest part of the submerged portion of the hull.

Most kayaks have a Cp between 0.45 and 0.60. Cp is important because of its relationship to hull resistance and the boat's motion. A boat with very full ends, or a high Cp, will tend to "push" its bow and stern waves farther apart and toward the ends of the hull. As you remember, the farther apart the waves are, the faster the boat is capable of moving. Of course when the Cp gets too high the waves get too big, and too much energy is required to push them; we then have a barge. A kayak with very fine ends, a low Cp, won't make efficient use of its length to achieve a high hull speed because the bow and stern waves will be too close together; however, such a boat may be very efficient at low and medium speeds. Most designers don't actually calculate a kayak's Cp; instead, they rely on experience and a good eye to draw the proper balance of fullness and fineness in the ends.

A kayak's bow and stern must also have enough buoyancy to stay above water. When boats with low Cp's are paddled in steep seas, the ends tend to dig into the faces of the waves. This can cause broaching when paddling downwind and make the boat difficult to control in other circumstances. With fine-ended designs, the hull should flare above the waterline to increase the kayak's reserve buoyancy.

The designer must also decide where to place the boat's maximum beam. If the widest part is at or near the midpoint of the boat's length, the kayak is said to have a *symmetrical form*. When the maximum beam is forward of the midpoint, the boat has a *fish-form* hull; if it is aft of center, the boat has a *swede-form* hull.

It's thought that the fish-form and symmetrical hulls are more efficient than swede-form designs, but the difference, if any, is slight. You've probably noticed that many modern kayaks appear to be swede-form. Because a boat's bow overhang is usually much longer than its stern overhang, the maximum waterline beam of a symmetrical-form boat may be aft of the center of its overall length, causing it to appear to be a swede-form. Some designers prefer to place the maximum beam aft of the cockpit so that the paddle will more easily clear the deck. Also, many paddlers prefer the appearance of a swede-form boat; perhaps this is a reaction to the shape of some racing kayaks that are built to specific measurement rules, giving them the swede-form.

Wetted-Surface Area

The *wetted-surface area* is the area of the hull below the waterline. At low speeds, the friction of the hull's skin is a greater source of resistance to forward progress than the waves formed by the kayak's forward motion. So a long, narrow boat with a high theoretical hull speed but a large wetted surface requires more energy to paddle at low speed than a short, fat boat with a minimal wetted surface. Paddlers sometimes buy long kayaks thinking they'll be able to go faster; for short bursts they will, but at normal touring speeds they may actually end up moving slower than in a shorter boat with less wetted-surface area.

The kayak on the left has less initial stability and less volume than the boat on the right; however, the kayak on the right also has a larger wetted-surface area.

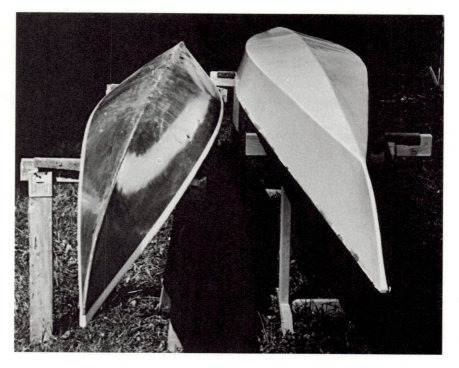

Boats with a very low wetted-surface area have cross sections resembling a semicircle; these hulls have very low initial stability. In extreme cases, such as flat-water racing kayaks, they can only be handled by expert paddlers. Touring-kayak hulls have flatter cross sections to increase initial stability, which adds wetted-surface area. Hard-chine and flat-bottomed boats have higher wetted-surface areas; however, they also tend to have larger load-carrying capacities—and that may be more important on long trips.

Volume

A kayak's volume is sometimes expressed in gallons or in cubic feet, but more often as high, medium, or low. Volume is influenced by a kayak's length, beam, prismatic coefficient, and depth or deck height. A high-volume kayak is one that holds tons of gear and a big paddler. For long-distance touring, you'll need to have sufficient volume to pack camping gear and supplies. A high-volume boat is usually slower and heavier than one with low or medium volume, but it is also drier and more comfortable. In strong winds, a high-volume kayak, with more freeboard, will be more difficult to control than a boat with a lower profile and lower volume.

Physical size is also important in choosing your kayak's volume. If you have a small build, you may feel uncomfortable or "lost" in a high-volume boat. You may also lack the weight to effectively lean such a boat. Larger paddlers often feel cramped in low-volume kayaks. Unless you plan extended trips or are particularly heavy or tall, there's little reason to choose a very high-volume kayak.

Rocker and Rudders

Rocker is the upward curve of the kayak's keel line over its length. If you place a kayak with pronounced rocker, such as a whitewater kayak, on a flat floor, the middle of the keel will touch the floor while the ends (at the waterline) will be several inches above the floor. Such a boat will turn easily but be difficult to paddle in a straight line. If a boat without any rocker is placed on the same floor, it will touch the floor over most of its length. This kayak will be difficult to turn but easy to paddle straight.

Tracking is more important than turning ability in touring and sea kayaks. To strike a balance between tracking and turning, most sea kayaks are designed with a small amount of rocker—one to three inches. Longer boats, boats with V-shaped hulls, or with very fine ends can have more rocker without compromising tracking. Also, a kayak with rocker is easier to maneuver in rough water. It's a common misconception that adding rocker makes a boat slower: actually, modern flat-water racing kayaks often have considerable rocker.

In heavy winds and seas, rudders are invaluable. They are also useful in doubles and in heavily loaded singles. Any kayak that must rely on a rudder to be handled properly, however, is unsafe. Rudders and skegs shouldn't be used as a remedy for poorly designed hulls. A boat that's deficient in tracking or turning can have a rudder added, but why not design it properly in the first place? A movable skeg can also be used to balance a boat in rough conditions, as illustrated by Frank Goodman's fine designs, and a skeg is far simpler to design and install. Rudders can and do fail, so they should be considered a convenience, not an essential.

Deck and Cockpit

The deck is an integral part of a kayak's design. It adds enormous rigidity and strength to the hull. A deck must have sufficient *camber*, or curvature, to accommodate the paddlers knees, feet, and gear. Camber increases a kayak's volume and allows the deck to quickly shed water and keep the paddler drier. A kayak with a cambered or peaked deck is easier to Eskimo roll. Decks that are too high, however, increase windage and make the boat more difficult to handle in extreme weather conditions.

Many plywood kayak decks are composed of flat, as opposed to cambered, sections. Such decks often have a tendency to flex or "oil-can." Most are designed with the mistaken belief that they are easier to build than curved decks. In fact, cambered decks are often simpler to construct and are usually lighter and stronger.

A kayak's cockpit must fit the paddler; it must be both snug and comfortable. Cockpits and seats can be customized with closed-cell foam padding, such as Ethafoam. The cockpit opening should allow the paddler to enter and exit the boat quickly and efficiently, though it must not be so wide or long that the paddler's knees can't be braced under the deck.

A sea kayak's coaming must be strong enough and low enough to sit on when performing a wet reentry. However, if the kayak is to be used primarily in calm water and without a spray skirt, then the coaming may be higher to help keep the paddler dry. In this case, the coaming doesn't have to be so heavily built because wet reentries are rare in calm-water paddling.

Choosing a Design

As you consider an existing design or draw your own, remember that any design is a compromise. It's relatively easy to design a boat that's well suited to one specific purpose—a very fast boat, for example, or one that's capable of carrying heavy loads. But designing a boat that can do several things well, that's an art.

By comparing a new design to kayaks you've paddled, you can get a fair idea of how it will suit you. But don't get hung up on "numbers"—you'll never notice an extra inch or two of length or a ¼ inch more rocker. If the design is 90 percent right, build it and go paddling.

All else aside, I've found that prettier boats are better boats. If you look at a new design and it doesn't move you, if it isn't a kayak that'll bring a smile to your face whenever you see it sitting on the beach, then it isn't the boat for you.

Plans

One of the great pleasures of boatbuilding is deciding which boat to build. You can spend many happy hours looking through back issues of *WoodenBoat* magazine, *Boatbuilding, messing about in Boats*, old issues of *Small Boat Journal* (sadly *Small Boat Journal* is all powerboats now, and its name has changed), and other magazines, looking at various kayak designs and advertisements for plans. But sooner or later it's time to send off a check and unroll your plans. If you're new to boatbuilding, the plans may seem complicated and confusing. But most boat plans are drawn in a similar style. Once you get the hang of reading one set of plans, you'll be able read most others as easily as you're reading this book.

Reading Plans

Traditionally, a set of plans for a small boat offers three views. There is a *profile view* showing the boat from the side; a *half-breadth*, or *plan, view* displaying the boat from the top; and a *body plan*, or *sections*, showing a combination front and back view. A set of lines resembling and serving the same purpose as contour lines on a map may be superimposed over these views; these are descriptively called the boat's lines. Boatbuilders measure and scale up these lines to full size using a process called *lofting*. Many designers also include a table of measurements from the centerline to the edge of the hull at particular cross sections. These are called *stations*, and the table is called the *table of offsets*. Offsets make the job of lofting far easier and faster.

Now if all this has you considering taking up bowling instead of kayak building, I have some good news. Most kayak plans drawn for amateur builders contain measurements for all the parts and don't require lofting or using tables of offsets. In many plan sets there are even full-size patterns for parts such as seats, footbraces, bulkheads, and coamings. Still, before you start building, it's important to study the boat's lines to know how the hull will be shaped.

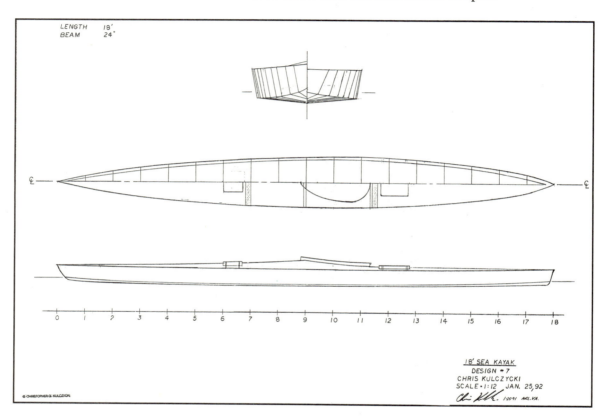

LENGTH 18'
BEAM 24"

18' SEA KAYAK
DESIGN #7
CHRIS KULCZYCKI
SCALE·1:12 JAN. 25,92

© CHRISTOPHER G. KULCZYCKI

This preliminary plan of a sea kayak consists of a body plan (top), a deck plan (middle), and a profile (bottom).

In addition to the main views of the boat, there will also be a few expanded views in the plans. Like close-ups, these show additional details. They are usually self-explanatory but are critical to understanding how the boat goes together. There will usually be sketches of the seat, hatches, footbraces, and other little parts that would only crowd the main drawing if they were detailed on the primary views.

In addition to the plan sheets, you'll need the *scantlings* and/or the bill of materials. The scantlings tell what material each part is made of, and the bill of materials tells you what will be needed. On kayak plans, both lists may be combined or the scantlings may be incorporated into the building directions. Study the bill of materials carefully so you can estimate that other important bill: your bill *for* materials.

Reproduced in Chapter 5 are the plans for three kayaks. These plans, like most published in books and magazines, are reduced from full size to fit on these pages; thus, they lose some clarity and detail. When you decide to build a particular kayak, you should invest in a full-size set of plans from the designer. It's certainly possible to build boats from plans reproduced in books and magazines, but having the full-size set and accompanying instructions will save you many hours and doubts, especially if you are a novice builder. The few extra dollars you spend will be forgotten when the boat is finished.

Modifying Plans

All paddlers have their own ideas of the perfect boat. One of the great advantages of building a boat is that your personal wants and needs can be accommodated. Modifications, if they are well thought out, will make the boat ideally suited to your paddling style. But before deciding on a design change, consider that a boat's designer has put substantial thought and experience into his design, so you should think carefully about any changes. Will they affect the strength of the kayak? Will it still be as seaworthy? If you put in a larger cockpit, for example, will the boat have less rigidity? Can you find a spray skirt to fit the cockpit? You may want a stronger boat and decide to increase the thickness of the hull skin, but the thicker wood might not conform to the desired shape. A better solution might be to add a layer of fiberglass cloth over the bottom. If the changes you want to make seem major or you're unsure of the effect they'll have on the boat's strength, then write to the designer for advice.

Designing Your Own Kayak

Many experienced paddlers are capable of designing their own kayaks, if they are willing to devote a fair amount of time and study to the task. If you choose to try your own design, consider starting with an existing design that you like and slowly redrawing it to meet your needs. Designing from a "blank sheet of paper" is much more difficult, and I wouldn't recommend trying it until you've built a few boats.

Scale Models

So you've designed the perfect kayak or found the perfect design, but you wish you could see a three-dimensional representation before you devote all that time to building it. Scale models have been used by designer's for almost as long as boats have been built. In fact, a traditional way to design a boat is to carve half the hull to scale (a half-model or half-hull) and to take measurements from it when drawing the boat's lines. Since you will be building plywood kayaks, it's only logical that you make plywood models.

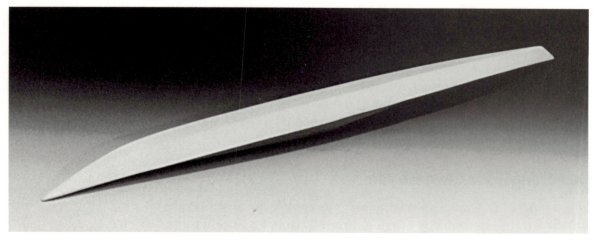

Boatbuilder and photographer Bob Grove built this handsome model of a sea kayak he was considering building.

The plywood to use is ⅟₃₂-inch or .8mm aircraft-grade birch. At a scale of one inch to one foot (a model of a 16-foot kayak is 16 inches long) the ⅟₃₂-inch plywood bends to about the same degree as 3mm or 4mm plywood does on a full-size boat.

The solid wood pieces should be made of bass or other soft wood. But you'll have to make the solid pieces a little thicker than the 1:12 scale calls for, or they won't be strong enough to support the plywood.

Slow-drying cyanoacrylate glue, which is available at hobby shops, should be used to hold the parts together. It is essentially a slow-drying version of Super Glue. It dries in several minutes, but if you're in a hurry, buy some accelerator to speed things up. I recommend this so you won't have to spend all night holding tiny little kayak parts together.

The fastest way to build a kayak model is to take your plans to a copy shop and have them reduced to a 1:12 scale. Now cut the pieces out of the copy and tape them to the $\frac{1}{32}$-inch plywood. Cut the plywood parts out with a pair of scissors and the solid parts with an X-acto knife and small saw. Glue everything together just as you would the real boat. Use masking tape, paper clips, and alligator clips for clamps.

When all else is equal, choose the prettier boat.

By building a model first, you'll gain valuable insights into how the real boat will be assembled and you'll have a good idea of how the finished version will look. Now carefully put your model away until it's time to varnish the full-size boat. Then take out the model and use it to bribe the neighbor's kid to stay away until the varnish dries.

Chapter 3
The Tools

At the Liberty Tool Company in Liberty, Maine, there are shelves upon shelves of old tools. Boxes and racks of ancient planes, saws, spokeshaves, drills, bevel squares, clamps, and hammers are jammed into every square foot of space. It smells of hardened steel, lubricating oil, and musty wood. I've spent happy hours combing the dusty recesses of each shelf and cabinet looking for hundred-year-old masterpieces ready to do duty again. I've wondered how many ships, houses, and boats these tools have created, and how many they have still to build.

Most of the tools at the Liberty Tool Company are good tools. The cheap tools, the discount specials, the homeowner-quality tools have long since been broken, bent, or rusted away. The tools on these shelves are the keepers—the sort of tools used by shipwrights, carpenters, jointers, cabinetmakers, and farmers who couldn't afford to waste money on cheap versions. They are the ones you should use to build your kayak.

Professional-quality tools are expensive and sometimes a challenge to find. But you'll need relatively few of them to build a kayak, so the extra cost isn't so much. And when your kayak is finished, the tools will still be ready for a lifetime or two of repairs and projects. In a few years their cost will be forgotten, but their quality and utility will be long appreciated by you and, many years later, by your grandchildren.

The differences between good tools and junk might be subtle: the type of steel used, the quality of the finish, the precision of the machining. The professional line of Stanley tools are of fine quality, as are brands like Record, Marples, Kunz, Sandvik, Jorgenson, and Bacho. One indication of a tool's quality is its price; another is where you find it. A professional cabinetmaker's supply house, for example, is not likely to carry junk.

Professional-quality power tools cost two to four times as much as homeowner-quality power tools. In exchange for steep prices, you'll get tools that stay adjusted, that you'll be able to find parts for, and that will probably last a lifetime. The only power tools you'll need are a sabersaw, a drill, and perhaps a small sander. Look for brands such as Porter Cable, Milwaukee, Makita, Bosch, AEG, and Hitachi—but be aware that some manufacturers of professional tools have introduced "homeowner" lines that aren't so well made.

As much as we may like to support local business, your neighborhood hardware store isn't the place to buy tools, nor is the local home-improvement store or department store. High-quality tools are made for professionals, so ask local boatbuilders, carpenters, or contractors where they buy their tools. You'll be amazed at how much you can learn and how much money you can save at a professional tool supplier. If you live in a small town where it's hard to find good tools, turn to some of the excellent mail-order discount-tool companies that advertise in *WoodenBoat* or *Fine Woodworking* magazines.

A list of tools you'll need or may want is on page 33. Most of these are readily available and used by carpenters or cabinetmakers. If you're familiar with traditional boatbuilding, you may be surprised by how few tools are required to build plywood kayaks. In the following section are a few thoughts and recommendations on some of the more important tools.

Tools for Measuring

Accurate measuring is critical to boatbuilding. The old adage "measure twice, cut once" is never truer than when applied to building boats. If your parts are accurately measured, they go together with little trouble. But sloppily measured pieces require fiddling, trimming, gap filling, and even swearing. The few minutes you save by measuring hurriedly will mean many more wasted minutes when it comes time to assemble—that I'll guarantee.

My measuring tools include a protractor, tapemeasure, chalkline, 36-inch rule, marking gauge, trammels, mechanical pencil, bevel square, and a 12-inch rule.

Before you start building, check all your measuring tools against each other. It's not uncommon to find a tape that doesn't agree exactly with a yardstick. I make all critical distance measurements with my tapemeasure or my metal 12-inch rule. I am certain that these are correct, so if there's any error I know who to blame.

The tool used more than any other will be your tapemeasure; Stanley and Lufkin make the best ones. The most durable and easiest to use are the 25-foot models with 1-inch-wide blades. The 30-foot x 1-inch tapes are also good, but their springs wear out sooner. Short, thin tapemeasures are best left for hanging pictures and building birdhouses.

I use a 12-inch metal rule divided into $\frac{1}{64}$-inch marks for measuring critical thicknesses like scarf lines, fastener lengths, drill-bit diameters, and other small dimensions. I also have a set of vernier calipers for critical measuring, but I'll admit that they're really overkill. You'll need a long rule to use as a straightedge; I use an inexpensive 36-inch steel drafting rule. For laying out longer lines, a piece of thin string or carpenter's chalkline is fine.

More measuring tools: a carpenter's square, a try square, and a nonessential vernier caliper.

In addition to tools for measuring distances, you'll need tools for measuring angles. A carpenter's square is needed to ensure right angles when you lay out the kayak's hull and deck panels. If you don't already have one, buy the large 24- x 18-inch version. A small 6-inch or 9-inch try square is handy for laying out and checking right angles in close quarters. The traditional boatbuilder's adjustable square, or bevel square, is also very useful—I wouldn't be without one. If you need to lay out radii, you can use a piece of string, but a set of trammels, which acts like a bar compass, makes the job easier. One last measuring device you'll want is a protractor; this can be a cheap, plastic student model, though larger versions are easier to read.

Once you've made a measurement, you'll need to mark it. Some craftsmen use only a knife or a scribe because they leave thinner lines than a pencil does. Actually, I prefer to use a sharp pencil as the line is easier to see. A mechanical pencil is wonderful because it never needs sharpening, but I'm always losing mine. A useful, though not essential, tool is a marking gauge. I use it to mark scarf lines and the position of the wire holes before stitching a hull together.

Tools for Cutting

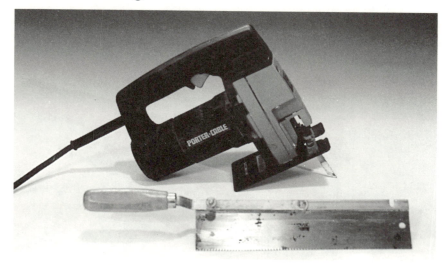

A sabersaw and a dovetail saw are essential.

The only power tool that you absolutely must have is a sabersaw. Sabersaws fall into one of two categories. There are expensive, heavy-duty professional models, and there are inexpensive, low-quality homeowner models. Though you certainly don't need the power of a professional model to cut the light materials needed for kayak building, the higher quality construction and superior blade guides on professional models make them a better choice. I use a top handle Porter Cable sabersaw that I'm quite fond of; Bosch and Hitachi also make fine sabersaws. Many boatbuilders prefer sabersaws without handles, called barrel-grip models, because they are a bit easier to control. Stay away from saws with a scroll feature; the scroll mechanism will eventually loosen, and the blade will wander and twist. Be sure any sabersaw you buy has a little blower to clear sawdust away from the blade so you can see what you're cutting. Another essential feature is a blade guide, mounted either on or just above the saw's base plate. Without this feature, the blade will tend to wander and bend as you're cutting through thick materials.

The best sabersaw blades are the bimetal type. They're often painted white, and they cost more than regular blades, but since you'll only wear out one or two blades per kayak, the additional cost is minimal. I use woodcutting blades with 10 teeth per inch.

A small handsaw is essential for accurate cuts in solid pieces. My favorite is a little Swedish dovetail saw made by Sandvik. It has a reversible, offset handle, so it can make flush cuts to either side. However, any small backsaw, tenon saw, or dovetail saw will do. Many boatbuilders and cabinetmakers are switching to a Japanese-style backsaw called a *dozuki*. They do cut incredibly fast; when my Sandvik wears out. . . .

Sooner or later you have to face the fact that some kayak parts need to be ripped from solid wood. The only tool for that job is a table saw. But unless you plan to build a lot more than one kayak, the cost of a table saw is prohibitive. Instead, arrange to use a friend's saw or pay a lumberyard to rip the sheer clamps, carlins, and other solid wood pieces. Actually, with a bit of searching, you might find the right size pieces already cut at a lumberyard.

A circular saw is useful for cutting boards to length and splitting sheets of plywood. But rather than get out my heavy old worm-drive saw, I'll often reach for a crosscut saw or a sabersaw instead. They don't cut as accurately, but most pieces will be fine-trimmed later.

Planes and Chisels

On the left is a Stanley model 220 block plane. On the right is the slightly better model 60½. A couple of chisels are also nice to have.

Woodworkers love planes, so you might be disappointed when I tell you that only a block plane is needed to build these kayaks. In fact, a block plane is likely to become your favorite tool. You'll use it to cut scarfs, to trim hull and deck panels, to clean up rough edges, and to shape small parts.

Block planes are available in standard models with an angle of about 20 degrees between the blade and the work surface and in low-angle models with an angle of 12 degrees to 13 degrees. The low-angle type is better suited to the cross-grain planing usually required in kayak building. I use a Stanley model 60½ low-angle plane; Record makes a similar plane (the Record 60½) that's a little better finished. If you already own a standard block plane, there's no need to buy a low-angle version; I used an old Stanley model 220 for years, until I dropped and cracked it.

You could certainly build a kayak without any chisels, but considering their usefulness and low cost it would be false economy. A ½-inch or ¾-inch cabinetmaker's chisel is all that you'll need. If kept very sharp, chisels can be used to trim pieces for that perfect fit. I also have a set of cheap Chinese chisels that I use for scraping glue and for other tasks that would ruin my good chisels.

Planes and chisels must be kept razor sharp to work properly. A dull plane will gouge and cause tear-outs. A dull chisel is dangerous to the boat and to the user. Buy a whetstone or water stone and use it often. If you can afford an electric water-stone sharpener, don't hesitate to get one; my little Wen electric sharpener is one of my most appreciated tools.

Staplers

Okay, this is not a traditional boatbuilder's tool. But when you need to temporarily clamp large, awkward plywood pieces, no other tool is as useful. If you fill it with stainless steel, Monel, or bronze staples, they can be left in the wood. If you think that the staples will spoil the finish, they are easy to remove and the tiny holes left behind are easy to fill. My stapler is an Arrow T-50 filled with ⅜-inch stainless steel staples.

Clamps

To build the kayaks in this book, you'll need at least 10 clamps, but 25 would not be too many. Most of them can be the old-fashioned C-clamps. Those operations that require the most clamps, gluing the cockpit coaming and the sheer clamps, can be accomplished with small 2-inch C-clamps. These can be bought from professional tool-supply companies very cheaply, so there's no excuse for running out. A few 2-inch spring clamps are also nice to have around for those times when you've only one free hand.

Light-duty bar clamps, like the popular orange Jorgensens, are the most useful large clamps. Every boatbuilder should own a couple of these in the 6-inch and 18-inch sizes. With practice they can be operated one-handed. A couple of 36-inch bar clamps or pipe clamps are handy for holding deck beams in place. Some larger C-clamps or heavy-duty 6-inch bar clamps should round out your clamp collection.

You can never have too many clamps. The little C-clamps near the top of the photo are inexpensive and most useful.

Oil or wax the clamp's threads, and they won't become fouled with epoxy. You'll often need a clamp in a hurry, so hang them all from a shelf or horizontal bar within easy reach of your work area. There are few things more frustrating than trying to untangle a pile of clamps while your carefully aligned parts slide apart.

Sanders

Sanding, like taxes, is one of the unpleasant realities of life. Compared to cold-molded or strip-planked boats, plywood kayaks

On the left is my Porter Cable random-orbital sander. It's a little faster than my reliable old Makita quarter-sheet finishing sander on the right.

don't require much sanding. You could do all that's required by hand in a few hours. Still, most of us will choose to use an electric sander.

My favorite is the quarter-sheet Makita palm sander. Many other companies make similar models, but the Makita fits my hand just right. It also sands fast enough that I can see progress, but not so fast that I accidentally sand through layers of plywood or fiberglass tape. Lately, I've been using a 5-inch random-orbital finishing sander from Porter Cable. It's a bit faster than my Makita, but it uses more expensive self-adhesive paper.

I also own a 3- x 21-inch belt sander for shaping small parts. To use it, I clamp it upside down to my workbench. If you're in a hurry, a belt sander is useful, but be forewarned that one slip and you could ruin a perfectly good kayak.

Drills

You could get by with almost any drill, including an old-fashioned eggbeater type. I use a light-duty, rechargeable Skil professional model with a built-in clutch. You don't need much drilling power to build these kayaks, so cordless drills are fine. In fact, they're almost addictive. The clutch is useful when driving screws because it prevents them from being over-driven.

You'll need a set of drill bits. Cheap drill bits bend, break, and dull quickly—they're not worth having. Instead consider a small but high-quality set of brad-point bits. Buy an extra $\frac{1}{16}$-inch bit because that's the size you'll use for wire-tie holes.

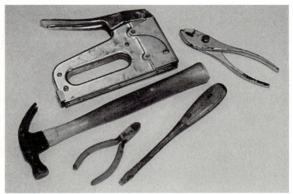

Miscellaneous Tools

Other tools you'll need include a set of screwdrivers, a pair of pliers, a pair of side cutters, a small hammer for driving ring nails (if you plan to use them), and a pair of scissors. Tools you may not need, but are handy to have, include a wooden mallet for tapping your chisel and a paint scraper for fast removal of epoxy drips.

Finally, don't start work until you have a pair of safety glasses and a respirator.

A light-duty rechargeable drill is handy to have.

A stapler, pliers, a small hammer, side-cutters, and a screwdriver round out the tool selection.

Setting Up Shop

You don't need a fancy shop to build a kayak; in fact, on nice days I often move my work outside. What you do need is a space a few feet longer and at least 6 feet wider than the kayak you're building. Your garage, basement, attic, or shed will do if it has sufficient light, ventilation, and electrical power. Many woodworkers already have fully equipped shops that are too short for building a long kayak. In this case, make all the pieces in the shop, then assemble the kayak outside and move it into your hallway or living room at night.

Good light is essential when building a kayak; you must be able to judge curves, joints, and surface quality entirely by eye. And you must be certain that the almost colorless epoxy resin is evenly and completely spread over the surfaces to be joined. If your shop isn't well lit, buy a cheap 48-inch fluorescent-light fixture, hang it from the rafters or ceiling, and your problem will be solved.

Safety glasses and a respirator—don't start work without them.

Building the kayaks in this book involves working with epoxy resins, varnish, paint, and acetone. In addition, copious quantities of sawdust are produced. Breathing in these fumes and particles is both unhealthy and unpleasant. Your shop must have enough doors or windows for good ventilation. If it doesn't, or if you're building during winter, install an exhaust fan. This can simply be a household fan set on a window sill. In any case, use your respirator.

Professional power tools draw considerable amperage. If your shop's electrical power is supplied by an extension cord be sure it's rated for the job. Any extension cord used with these tools should be of at least 14-gauge wire (12-gauge is better); the longer the cord is the more crucial heavy wire becomes. Your tools will still operate if you use a thin cord, but they'll overheat and might burn out.

Epoxy resin should be used within a certain temperature range. During winter or on cold nights, your shop should be heated. In my small, uninsulated shop two portable electric heaters provide sufficient warmth on all but the coldest nights. On very cold nights, you can make a "tent" over your boat from a plastic tarp and aim a heater under it.

Equip the shop with a sturdy set of sawhorses to hold your kayak. Pad the tops of the sawhorses with pieces of scrap carpet, so the boat won't get scratched. You'll need a workbench or table to lay out your plans and to make and assemble smaller parts. Much of kayak building involves just sitting and thinking, so think about getting a stool or chair for your shop.

Building a strong pair of sawhorses is a good tune-up project. Pad the tops with a scrap of carpet.

Tool List

Tools You Need

Tapemeasure
12-inch ruler
Carpenter's square
String line
Protractor
Pencils
Long straightedge
Sabersaw
Drill and bits
Block plane
Screwdrivers
Handsaw
Clamps (at least 10)
Stapler
Pliers
Side cutters
Small hammer
Saw horses

Tools You May Want

More clamps
Electric sander
Table saw
Circular saw
Spokeshave
Chisels
Mallet
Marking gauge
Try square
Bevel square
Paint scraper
Trammels

Chapter 4
The Materials

T he resurgence of wooden-boat building is due largely to the development of modern plywood and epoxy resins. The kayaks described in this book aren't really wooden boats in the traditional sense; they are more accurately described as wood-epoxy composite construction. Epoxy gives these boats many of the qualities we associate with modern plastics: strength, durability, and resistance to corrosion and rot. Plywood frees us from the difficulties of finding long pieces of high-quality lumber and from the sometimes inconsistent strength of natural wood, yet it has wood's light weight, strength, and resiliency. And plywood can be worked with ordinary and affordable tools.

The cost of the materials that make up a kayak are only a small fraction of the value of the time you'll devote to the project. Don't scrimp on materials—buy the best you can afford. Your savings over the price of a finished boat will still be substantial. Good materials, like good tools, are more enjoyable to work with, and when your kayak is launched you won't worry about its integrity or its durability.

Plywood

Plywood is manufactured from thin sheets of wood, called *veneers,* which are cut from a tree trunk. These veneers are stacked and glued together to form the plywood panel. There are between three and 11 layers of veneer in a sheet of normal plywood. The kayaks described in this book are built using 3- or 4mm-thick plywood made from three layers of veneer.

Unlike solid wood, the strengths, bending characteristics, and quality of plywood panels are predictable and very consistent. Various systems have been developed to grade plywood, but you can easily judge its quality yourself. Ask if the plywood is made with phenolic (waterproof) glue; reject any that isn't. Look for voids in the plywood's inner plys. These can be spotted along the edges of the panels; don't use any plywood containing voids. Next, examine the panel's surfaces for repairs made with wood plugs or putty. You can decide how you want your boat to look, but I'll pass over any panels that have wood-plug repairs or more than a touch of putty. If you want

Plywood, whether thick or thin, should have plies of approximately equal thickness and no voids.

further proof of quality, look for Lloyd's Register of Shipping Approval or for panels that meet British Standard 1088. The finest plywood panels come from European manufacturers such as Shelman, Bruynzeel, Lydney, and Toubois. The panels are uniform in quality, free of voids and surface repairs, and not prone to delamination. The best of these are very expensive, but there are less expensive, though perfectly serviceable, grades available.

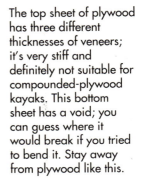

The top sheet of plywood has three different thicknesses of veneers; it's very stiff and definitely not suitable for compounded-plywood kayaks. This bottom sheet has a void; you can guess where it would break if you tried to bend it. Stay away from plywood like this.

Plywood that's suitable for kayak construction can be manufactured from one of several different species of wood. I prefer to use plywood made from *okoume*, an African hardwood similar in texture to mahogany but a little lighter in both weight and color; it's also known as *Gaboon*. Okoume is very light, easy to bend, and easy to work with hand tools. It takes a beautiful paint or varnish finish and readily absorbs epoxy. Okoume is not regarded to be a very durable wood, so care must be taken to completely coat it with epoxy, particularly the panel's edges. But claims about the relative durability of woods are not always accurate. Some scraps of unfinished 3mm okoume plywood have been lying in the grass outside my shop for 18 months; they do not show the slightest sign of rot or delamination—despite okoume's reputation for low durability.

Okoume marine-grade panels are made in thicknesses from 3mm to 18mm. Since they're manufactured in Europe, they are often 125cm x 250cm in size (or about 4 feet 1½ inches x 8 feet 2½ inches), though they are sold as 4- x 8-foot sheets. Some kayak plans, including the Yare (see plans in Chapter 5), are drawn to take advantage of those extra few inches, so check to see if the panels you are buying are metric or American sized. Okoume plywood 4mm or thicker is sometimes available in 5- x 10-foot panels that are very useful when building doubles or longer single kayaks.

In addition to marine-grade okoume panels there are 3mm exterior-grade okoume sheets, called *bending panels*. These are intended for pattern work and cold molding, but they are also suitable for kayak building. The surface quality of exterior-grade okoume plywood varies with the manufacturer. Better quality bending panels are almost indistinguishable from marine grade, though others must be sanded and painted. Bending panels cost one-third to one-half as much as marine grade and are usually metric sized. Obviously, they're an attractive option for building prototypes and first projects, or for reducing costs.

Lauan is also called Philippine mahogany, though it's not a true mahogany at all. It is, however, a fairly strong, rot-resistant, and attractive wood. Lauan plywood has gained widespread acceptance in amateur boatbuilding. Exterior-grade Lauan plywood is sold by most commercial lumberyards in ⅛-inch (about 3mm) thick panels, called "doorskins," and in ¼-inch (about 6mm) thick panels, called "underlayment." The ⅛-inch lauan can be substituted for 3mm okoume when building compounded-plywood kayaks but at a cost in appearance and perhaps durability. One-quarter-inch lauan plywood is manufactured with a thick end-grain core sandwiched between two thinner veneers. These panels are very stiff and are unsuitable for bending. This stiffness, however, makes them ideal for bulkheads, cockpit rims, and small parts.

The quality of exterior-grade lauan panels varies widely, so examine each panel carefully before buying. (If this isn't possible, at least the price is so low that you may not be too bothered by the occasional flawed panel.) Remember that exterior-grade panels take more time to finish than the better-made marine grade, so you'll lose in time what you'll have saved in cost.

One last warning about exterior-grade lauan panels: Be careful that you are buying sheets of the same thickness. For instance, a friend bought some panels to build two kayaks for his teenaged sons. One of these panels was damaged, so he returned to the same lumberyard a few weeks later to buy a replacement. He cut all the pieces out, stitched and taped the hulls together, and was starting to form the hulls when he noticed that the new piece of wood was thicker and would not bend as the others had. Though the sheet was sold as identical to the others, it was about 20 percent thicker. Buyer beware.

Lauan plywood is also manufactured in marine grade. It's a much higher and more consistent quality than the exterior grade. Even with marine grade, however, only plywood with veneers of uniform thickness should be used in compounded-plywood boats.

Sapele is an African mahogany often used in making marine-grade plywood panels. I've built one kayak using sapele plywood, and I found it to be a little stiffer and harder to work than okoume. However, sapele has a wonderful rich red color, and it's said to be more durable than okoume. Sapele is a little more expensive than other mahoganies, but I wouldn't hesitate to recommend it if appearance is paramount. Another African mahogany sometimes seen in marine-grade panels is *khaya*. Though I have had little experience with it, I have heard good reports from other boatbuilders. It's certainly a handsome, dark-brown wood, and it's reputed to be fairly durable.

I'm often asked about using teak plywood for kayak construction. While teak is undeniably a lovely wood and is probably the most durable of any species, it has limited applications in kayak building. What makes teak so durable is its high oil content; unfortunately, this oil also makes teak difficult to glue. Teak is best left as solid wood for use as trim on your kayak.

All domestic marine-grade plywood is made from Douglas fir, a superb, solid wood; it is light, strong, and durable. Unfortunately, it makes a poor plywood for kayak hulls. Because Douglas fir grows in temperate regions, it has different growth rates during different seasons; thus, it also has different rates of expansion and contraction, which means the wood is prone to checking or splitting. Additionally, the nature of fir and the quality standards of American plywood manufacturers combine to make this plywood unattractive and difficult to finish. Fir plywood can be used for coaming spacers, bulkheads, and other parts where bending properties and appearance aren't important. For these applications, exterior grade is sufficient.

There are a number of other marine, aircraft, and exterior-grade plywood panels available. Generally, if they contain veneers of equal thickness, waterproof glue, and don't have voids in the core plies, they are probably suitable for kayak construction.

Solid Wood

Though the hulls of the kayaks in this book are plywood, many of the internal parts are made from solid wood. Most of the solid wood used in a kayak will be ripped into thin strips for frames, sheer clamps, and small parts. So you won't need the large high-quality boards used in traditional boatbuilding. Short pieces of wood can easily be joined with scarf joints to make up the longer lengths you'll need. Because all the wood in a kayak is protected by epoxy, varnish, or paint, and the boats are not left in the water for long periods of time and are stored under cover, you don't have to be too concerned about the durability of the solid woods.

Most of the solid wood in your kayak will be ripped into thin strips. So the long, wide planks common to traditional boatbuilding are not necessary.

Spruce, whether Sitka spruce or eastern spruce, is the best choice for parts that must be strong, stiff, and light, such as sheer clamps and keelsons. Sitka spruce has long been prized for sailboat masts and airplane parts because it's available in long, clear lengths. However, today it's expensive and difficult to find. Eastern spruce, though not usually clear, is readily found in most lumberyards as dimensional lumber for home building. If you take the time to sort through a pile of good-quality eastern spruce, you'll find enough clear pieces to build a kayak and pay far less than you would have for Sitka spruce. I usually buy Eastern spruce in 1- x 4-inch x 16-foot lengths then rip it to width. It's hard to find 16-foot lengths that are entirely free of knots, but they are cheap enough that I simply discard strips containing more than one tight knot.

Douglas fir, or Oregon pine, runs a close second to spruce as my choice of solid wood; in fact, if the fir is exceptionally good quality, I'll choose it over spruce. Douglas fir is a little heavier than spruce but somewhat stronger. It is easy to find at lumberyards, where long, clear boards are common. The grain of Douglas fir varies considerably, so look through a pile to find the best pieces; try to select boards that are lightweight but have straight, tight grain. The main disadvantage of Douglas fir is its brittleness. The wood has a tendency to crack when bent, and it may check if left exposed to the weather. Both Douglas fir and spruce absorb moisture readily if left unsealed, so don't leave your wood sitting out in the rain.

Cedar is another wood that's sometimes used in kayaks. There are several varieties of cedar; Alaska cedar, Oxford cedar, and white cedar are lightweight, soft woods suitable for sheer clamps, carlins, keelsons, and other parts. However, cedar isn't quite as strong as spruce or fir, so the parts should be made a little thicker. Western red cedar is the only species that should be avoided; it's simply not strong enough for structural uses.

Like many woodworkers, you may have a cache of mahogany, ash, clear pine, or other cabinet-grade lumber. There's no reason not to use these woods in your kayak, except that you may increase its weight and cost slightly. I enjoy adding a few trim pieces of exotic wood to enhance the appearance of a boat.

Epoxy

You'll use epoxy resin in several capacities when building your plywood kayak. It will be a glue to hold parts together, an adhesive for fiberglass tape, a coating to protect and waterproof bare wood, and a gap filler and fairing compound. Epoxy is strong, easy to use, forgiving, and totally waterproof; it's boatbuilding's version of a miracle drug. Several companies market epoxy systems consisting of various resins, hardeners, and application tools. Read their catalogs before buying your epoxy.

Epoxy is sold in two parts: the resin and a hardener. The ratio of resin to hardener varies among brands of epoxy; it's critical that the two are mixed precisely to the manufacturer's instructions. Since epoxy resin and hardener are extremely sticky, using measuring cups to mix them is both inaccurate and unpleasant. Most epoxy manufacturers sell small, inexpensive plastic pumps that screw into the tops of the resin and hardener cans and precisely meter the liquids. To mix the epoxy, hold a disposable container under the nozzles and simply push down on each pump. The epoxy and hardener will be dispensed at the exact ratio required, and you'll only have to give them a stir. If you can't find metering pumps, try using the disposable plastic measuring cups available from medical supply houses.

My epoxy table—everything I need is at hand. Notice the epoxy-metering pumps and the various thickeners; this should excite you closet chemists out there.

Epoxy resin is thinner than most glues and will flow out of gaps and joints unless it's first mixed with a thickening agent or filler. Epoxy manufacturers sell many types of thickening agents. I prefer chopped-cotton fibers (sold by Evercoat) or plastic minifibers (sold by System Three). Many boatbuilders favor wood flour, which is basically fine sawdust, as a thickener because it more closely matches the color of the surrounding wood. However, wood flour tends to absorb the epoxy slowly, and it's difficult to predict just how thick the mixture will become. Wood flour will continue absorbing epoxy and might cause a joint to be dry and weak.

Most thickeners are intended to create a strong bond and so result in a fairly dense and heavy mixture. But for some applications, such as fairing or filleting, a light and easily sanded mixture is preferable to a strong, dense one. *Microspheres* are tiny, hollow plastic pellets that, when mixed with epoxy, provide a light adhesive mixture perfect for sanding. Microspheres are included in all the major epoxy systems. Another useful thickener is West System 404, a high-density and high-strength filler. It produces a very strong mixture that's useful for bonding rudder mounts, footbraces, and other hardware.

Epoxy, regardless of all its wonderful properties, needs reinforcement when used in highly stressed areas like hull seams. You could use keelsons, butt plates, and chine logs at the seams, but a far simpler and lighter solution is fiberglass tape to reinforce the seams. Fiberglass tape is nothing more than a strip of fiberglass cloth; it's not even sticky. When combined with a plastic resin, such as epoxy, it forms a tough and durable structure; that's basically how fiberglass kayaks are built, after all. Be sure to buy the selvage-type tape and not the sort with unfinished edges. Fiberglass tape may be available in various weights; I prefer 9-ounce tape. It's far more economical to buy tape in 50-yard rolls than by the yard.

Epoxy manufacturers also sell many special-purpose products to mix with resin. These include low- and high-temperature hardeners, graphite powder to produce low-friction surfaces and protect the resin from sunlight (normally, epoxy must be over-coated with paint or varnish), aluminum powder to increase surface hardness, fire-retardant filler, and others. I've used some of these products, but not long enough to recommend them. If you've always wanted a chemistry set, they may be the next best thing.

Having a few inexpensive accessories and supplies makes using epoxy systems much easier. In addition to the dispensing pumps and disposable mixing cups mentioned earlier, you should have stirring sticks, several pairs of disposable gloves, and an apron to keep the sticky stuff off your clothes. For applying epoxy, get disposable brushes, foam rollers, and a plastic squeegee or plastic putty knife. The only truly effective solvent for epoxy is acetone; get some for cleaning up.

Set up a tray or small table—that you don't have any other use for— and use it as your epoxy station. Having all your epoxy-related paraphernalia in one place makes building easier, and you can move it all out of the way after you're finished.

Several manufacturers market epoxy-resin systems formulated for marine woodworking. Over the years I've used West System, System Three, and Evercoat epoxies. I can't say that I prefer any of these brands over another; they all work well. If you work carefully and don't sheath the hull in fiberglass cloth, you'll need two to three quarts of epoxy to build a kayak. But a gallon container usually costs only a few dollars more than two quart-cans, and if you spill any you'll wish you'd spent the extra money.

Epoxy resins, hardeners, and solvents contain potentially dangerous chemicals. Avoid getting them on your skin; wear disposable gloves and use barrier cream. Don't use acetone to remove epoxy from your skin; use soap and water, vinegar, or waterless hand cleaner instead. Even though you might not smell them, epoxy emits fumes—so keep that window open. As epoxy cures, it gives off heat; several ounces of epoxy left sitting in a cup produces enough heat to crack a glass container or melt some types of plastic. Use paper or thick plastic cups for mixing epoxy, and be sure to pour any that's left over into a metal can.

Fasteners

Very few metal fasteners are needed in a plywood kayak. In fact, you could build one of these boats with no metal in it at all. Most kayaks, however, will contain a few screws, ring nails, and some copper wire.

Stainless steel comes in various grades, some of which are not very stainless at all; so, particularly if you'll be paddling in salt water, buy screws from a reputable marine dealer. Bronze ring nails can be used to help hold down the kayak's deck. (These are sometimes called boat nails.) Don't substitute brass or copper fasteners for bronze. They are not nearly as strong or as corrosion-resistant. And please, don't try to save a few cents by using steel or galvanized fasteners—wouldn't you feel foolish with big rust streaks down the side of your kayak? If you use staples, get stainless steel, Monel, or bronze, in case one breaks off in the wood or some aren't removed.

The other metal fastener that will be used is uninsulated copper wire for stitching the hull together. I prefer 18-gauge wire that is sold at many hardware stores for hanging birdfeeders and tying up roses. Copper is the best type of wire to use because it cuts easily and sands

(left) These are all the stainless steel fasteners that go into a kayak. Don't be a cheapskate and substitute brass or galvanized hardware.

(right) Copper wire is used to clamp the hull until the epoxy sets; bronze ring nails hold down the deck until the epoxy sets.

flush with the wood. Stainless steel wire is available but it's very stiff, hard to twist, and very difficult to sand. A few builders use heavy monofilament fishing line because it's almost invisible—but imagine tying all those knots.

Finding Materials

Going to most lumberyards and asking for okoume plywood will result in little more than a funny look from the salesperson. Marine plywoods, epoxies, and fasteners are all specialty items. If you don't live in a traditional boatbuilding area, you'll probably have to order some materials by mail. Ask local boatbuilders where they buy materials or look through the ads in *WoodenBoat* magazine for local sources. There's a list of suppliers who sell by mail in Appendix B.

Chapter 5
The Plans

I drew the plans for the three kayaks in this chapter for my own use. They're not perfect for everyone, but I'll make no excuses for that. I've always drawn plans for kayaks that I wanted to paddle, not necessarily for kayaks that I thought would sell well. I hope from reading my descriptions that you'll be able to judge if one of the kayaks is the sort of boat you want. To that end, I'll try to describe both their flaws and their attributes, but these are subjective. One last caveat: if you want a boat that's not drawn here, then do go out and find the plans or draw them for yourself. Never choose a kayak simply because the plans for it are in front of you, or because you don't want to spend a few dollars on plans for a boat you like better.

It can be frustrating trying to read plans if you're not used to it, or even if you are. I spent several years sitting in my office at a civil engineering firm answering questions from contractors and county inspectors who couldn't understand something in our plans. It drove me to building kayaks. Most people who draw plans really do try to make them easy to understand, but what's obvious to one person is often obtuse to another. Having a good clean set of full-size drawings, the accompanying instructions, and a little patience will answer most questions. Experience will answer many of the rest. The last few questions might require an answer from the designer.

"The ducks leave a bigger wake than the Yare," says one paddler after taking her out for a spin.

The Yare

I designed the predecessor of the Yare, the Skua 16, for the Winter '91 issue of *Sea Kayaker* magazine. Many readers built and enjoyed it.

But I wasn't fully satisfied with the Skua design, so I continued refining it and built several modified versions that culminated in the Yare. Hundreds of plan sets for the Yare have been sold; it's been my most popular design. At the risk of being immodest, I am not surprised by its popularity—consider its specifications: length, 16 feet 3 inches; beam, 24 inches; and a weight of only 25 to 30 pounds (depending on how it's fitted out). But the best thing about the Yare is how easily it paddles, which is the result of a fairly long waterline and narrow waterline beam, combined with a very low wetted-surface area.

The Yare probably shouldn't be considered a true sea kayak. Its low volume and fine ends mean a fairly wet ride in a chop, and it's hard to pack enough into its low hull for a trip of more than one or two nights. But it's capable of making coastal trips if you can accept those drawbacks. The rewards of paddling the Yare are in its speed and efficiency; at normal touring speeds, very little energy is required to move the boat. The Yare can be fitted with a rudder, but it tracks well enough without one.

The Yare is at its best on day trips on protected water. It's the sort of boat that's a joy to take down to the river or bay after work and paddle for a couple of hours. Its light weight means that it's not a chore to unload from a roof rack, even on windy days. Though the Yare's initial stability is lower than that of most kayaks, I've seen many novices handle it with no trouble.

The Yare is built from two sheets of European 3mm plywood. (It can easily be shortened a few inches to use American plywood.) It takes about 40 hours to build, not including painting or varnishing.

Bill of Materials

▼ 2 sheets 3mm okoume plywood (250 cm x 125 cm, or the Yare can be shortened by a few inches and built from 4- x 8-foot sheets)

▼ 3 x 2 feet of ¼-inch plywood

▼ 3 x 2 feet of ½-inch plywood

▼ 40 feet of ¾-inch square spruce or pine molding

▼ 12 feet of ¼- x 1¼-inch lattice or furring strips

▼ 3 quarts marine epoxy resin

▼ Thickening agent for epoxy

▼ 1 roll of 3-inch, 9-ounce fiberglass tape

▼ 1 pound of ¾-inch bronze ring nails

▼ 25 feet of copper wire (18-gauge is best)

▼ 8, #8, ¾-inch stainless steel wood screws and finish washers

▼ 8, 1½-inch, thin stainless steel sheet-metal screws

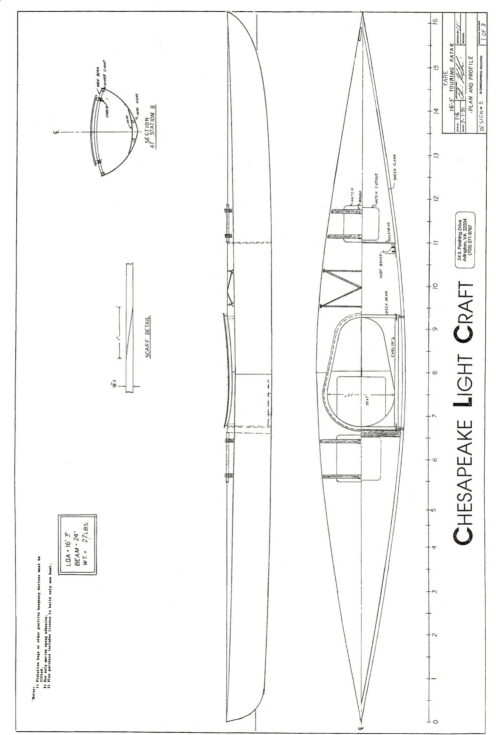

SECTION
AT STATION 8

SCARF DETAIL

LDA - 16' 3"
BEAM - 24"
WT. - 27 LBS.

Notes:
1) Flotation bags or other positive buoyancy devices must be
   fitted.
2) Use only marine epoxy adhesive.
3) Plan purchase includes license to build only one boat.

CHESAPEAKE LIGHT CRAFT

34 S. Pershing Drive
Arlington, VA 22204
(703) 271-8787

YARE
16'-3" TOURING KAYAK

PLAN AND PROFILE

DESIGN # 5

The following items are needed if you plan to install bulkheads and hatches:

▼ 8 feet of ¾- x ⅜-inch foam weatherstripping tape

▼ 4, 1-inch plastic Fastex buckles

▼ 14 feet of 1-inch nylon webbing

▼ 8, #8, ¾-inch stainless steel wood screws and finish washers

▼ 2 x 2 feet of 3-inch closed-cell foam or ¼-inch plywood for bulkheads

▼ 4 feet of 1- x ¼-inch lattice or lath

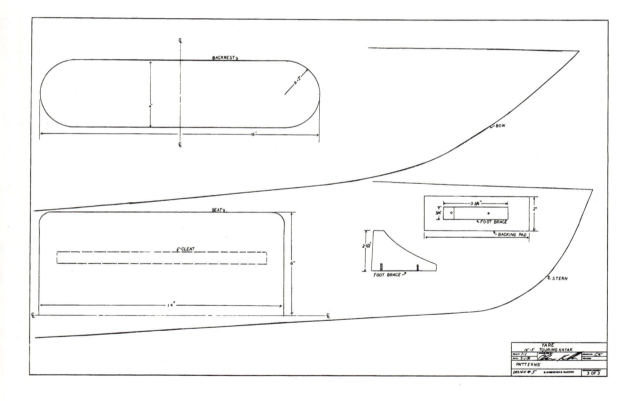

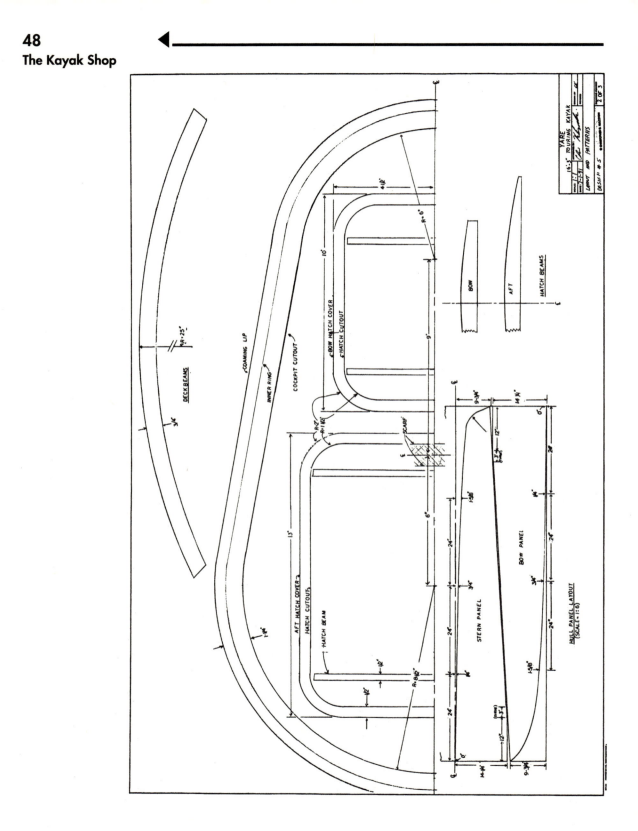

The Cape Charles

I designed the Cape Charles because I wanted a big, stable boat for long journeys, particularly for a trip to Newfoundland that I've been planning. The Cape Charles is an 18-foot hard-chine sea kayak. It has fairly high volume, high initial and secondary stability, and the capacity to handle large loads and large paddlers. I consider this a kayak suitable for coastal trips up to several weeks in length. The Cape Charles has a long waterline and thus a high hull speed. But because of its greater waterline beam, larger wetted-surface area, and hard-chine construction, it is not so effortless to paddle as the Yare.

The Cape Charles weighs about 40 pounds; that's about a third less than comparable fiberglass and plastic boats. It's designed to be fitted with a rudder, though it tracks well without one for most paddlers. With a lightweight paddler and no additional load, however, it won't sit down on its lines and must have a small, fixed skeg added or else it will be skittish. The Cape Charles would normally be fitted with hatches, bulkheads, and deck tie-downs.

This kayak is built of two sheets of 4m plywood and one of 3mm. Since the panels that form its hull don't bend much, the type of plywood you use is not so important. It can be built in about 60 hours,

The Cape Charles can handle heavy loads and long distances. This is the boat I paddle most often.

not including finishing. When I built this boat, I was surprised at how easily it went together. It is a little more labor intensive than a compounded-plywood boat, but there seems to be less mental work involved.

Bill of Materials

▼ 2 sheets of 4mm plywood (4 x 8 feet)
▼ 1 sheet of 3mm plywood (4 x 8 feet)
▼ 3 x 2 feet of ¼-inch plywood
▼ 3 x 2 feet of ½-inch plywood
▼ 40 feet of ¾-inch-square spruce or pine
▼ 17 feet of ¼- x 1¼-inch lattice
▼ 37 feet of ¼- x ¾-inch ash or other clear wood for rubrail
▼ 3 quarts of marine epoxy resin
▼ Thickening agent for epoxy
▼ 2 rolls of 3-inch, 9-ounce fiberglass tape
▼ 50 feet of copper wire (18-gauge is best)
▼ 8, #8, ¾-inch stainless steel wood screws and finish washers
▼ 8, 1½-inch thin stainless steel sheet-metal or wood screws
▼ 4 feet of 1-inch nylon strap
▼ 1 pound ¾-inch, 14-gauge bronze ring nails

The following items are needed if you plan to install bulkheads and hatches:

▼ 8 feet of 1-inch foam weatherstripping
▼ 4, 1-inch plastic Fastex buckles
▼ 14 feet of 1-inch nylon webbing
▼ 8, #8, ¾-inch stainless steel wood screws and finish washers
▼ 2 x 2 feet of 3-inch closed-cell foam or ¼-inch plywood for bulkheads
▼ 7 feet of ¼- x 1¼-inch lattice or lath

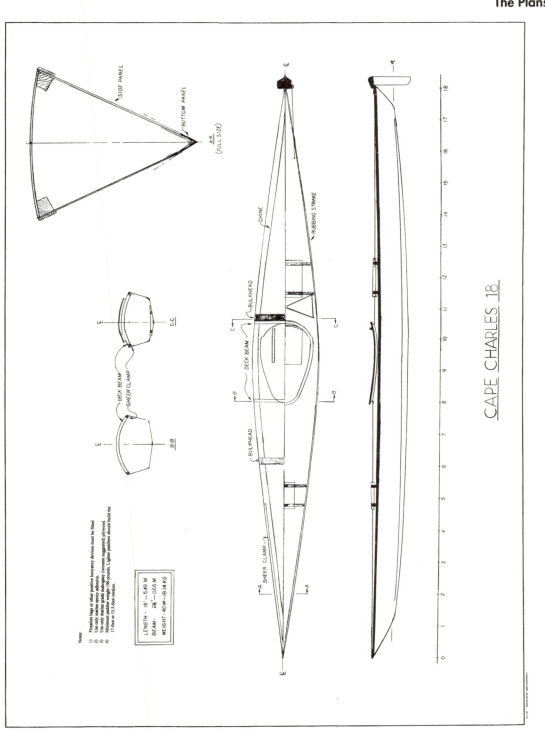

SIDE PANEL

BOTTOM PANEL

A-A
(FULL SIZE)

Notes:

1) Flotation bags or other positive buoyancy devices must be fitted
2) Use only marine epoxy adhesive.
3) Use only marine grade mahogany (occume suggested) plywood.
4) Minimum paddler weight 190 pounds. Lighter paddlers should build the 17-foot or 15.5-foot version.

LENGTH - 18' — 5.49 M
BEAM - 26" — 0.66 M
WEIGHT - 40# — 18.14 KG

DECK BEAM

SHEER CLAMP

C-C

B-B

CHINE

RUBBING STRAKE

BULKHEAD

DECK BEAM

BULKHEAD

SHEER CLAMP

CAPE CHARLES 18

0 1 2 3 4 5 6 7 8 9 10 11 12 13 14 15 16 17 18

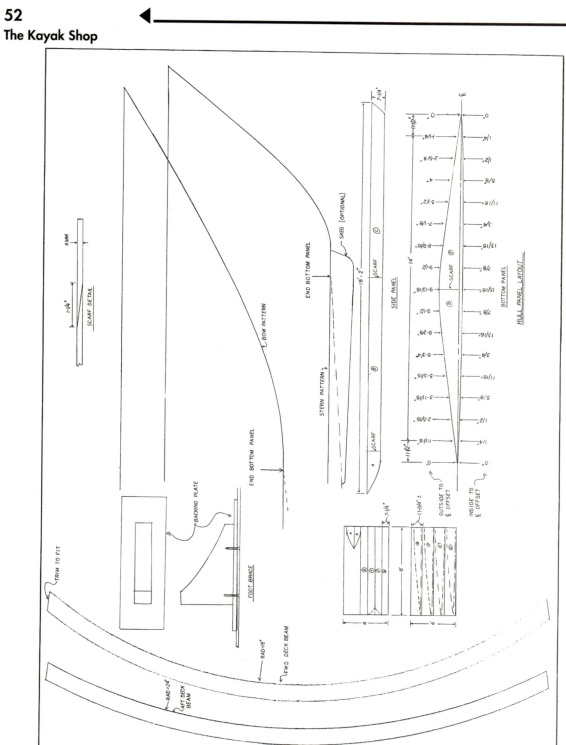

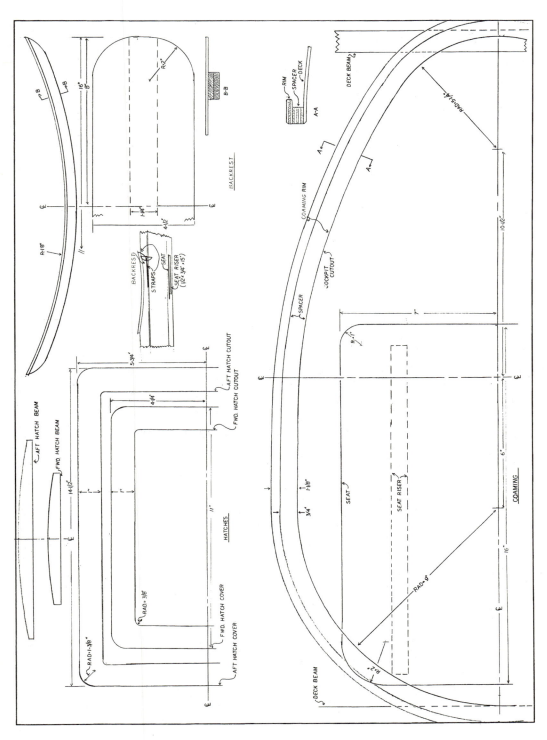

The Pocomoke

I generally don't like double kayaks; too often they are heavy, beamy, and slow. I do own a folding Klepper double and enjoy it very much, but I consider it more of a narrow sailboat than a kayak. In fact, I almost never use it without its sailing rig. The Pocomoke was designed as a lightweight double that could just as easily be paddled by one person. It's 19 feet 10 inches long, has a 28-inch beam, and weighs about 52 pounds, but those figures are deceptive because it has a relatively low volume. Construction is compounded plywood, very similar to that of the Yare.

The name "Pocomoke" is taken from a particularly beautiful river on the Chesapeake Bay's Eastern Shore. Long, winding, and narrow—it's just the sort of water this kayak is perfect for.

Many people who saw this boat liked it but wanted a fully decked version, which is more suitable for rough water. So I designed a two-cockpit deck for it; that plan is also reproduced here. A few builders have even built the Pocomoke as a single.

The Pocomoke is a single and a half, a small, fast double and a manageable single in one boat.

Because of the Pocomoke's low volume, it's not the ideal kayak for long trips with two people; like the Yare, it's better suited to day paddling.

The Pocomoke is best built from two 5- x 10-foot sheets of 4mm plywood. If these panels aren't available, the boat can be built from 4 x 8 sheets, but with significant wastage. Building time should be about 60 hours for an unvarnished hull. The hull is no harder to build than the Yare's, but the open cockpit does require a little more wood-working skill than the single type.

Bill of Materials

▼ 2 sheets of 5- x 10-foot 4mm marine-grade okoume plywood (or 4 sheets of 4- x 8-foot plywood)

▼ 1 x 3 inches x 10 feet of spruce or fir

▼ Two lengths of ⅜ inch x 3 inches x 8 feet of spruce or cedar, or 3 inches x 8 feet of ¼-inch plywood

▼ 18 feet of ½-inch half-round pine or spruce molding

▼ 60 feet of ½- x ¼-inch rectangular molding (mahogany preferable)

▼ 20 feet of ¼- x 1½-inch pine or spruce lath

▼ 4 feet of ¾-inch dowel (a broomstick!)

▼ 1- x 10-inch x 3-foot pine board

▼ 1 roll of 3-inch, 9-ounce fiberglass tape

▼ 3 quarts of marine epoxy resin

▼ Thickening agent for epoxy

▼ 1 pound of ¾-inch bronze ring nails

▼ 6, #10, 1-inch bronze wood screws and finish washers

▼ 10, #8, 1½-inch bronze wood screws

▼ box 1-inch brass finish nails

▼ 25 feet of 18-gauge brass wire

▼ pad eye for bow and stern

The following additional items are needed if you are installing bulkheads and hatches:

▼ 8 feet of foam weatherstripping

▼ 4, 1-inch plastic Fastex buckles

▼ 14 feet of 1-inch nylon webbing

▼ 8, #8, ¾-inch stainless steel wood screws and finish washers

▼ 2 x 3 feet of 3-inch closed cell foam or ¼-inch plywood for bulkheads

▼ 4 feet of 1- x 1½-inch lattice or lath

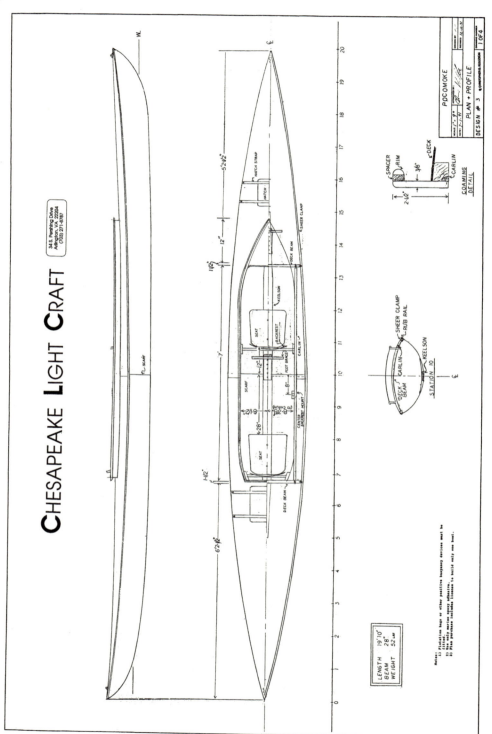

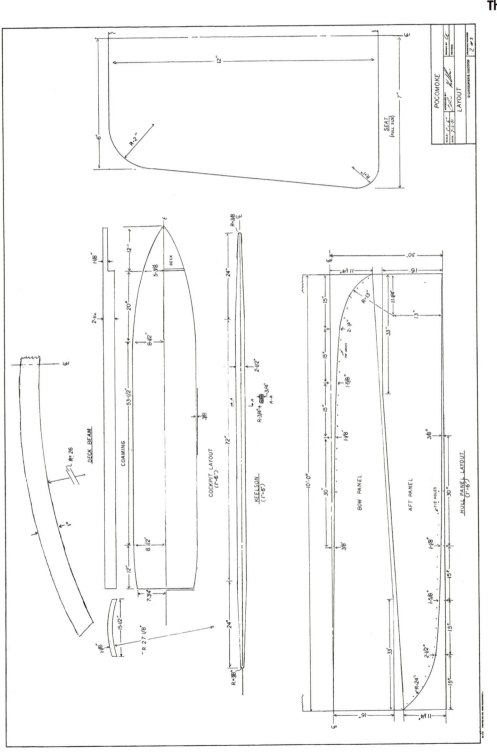

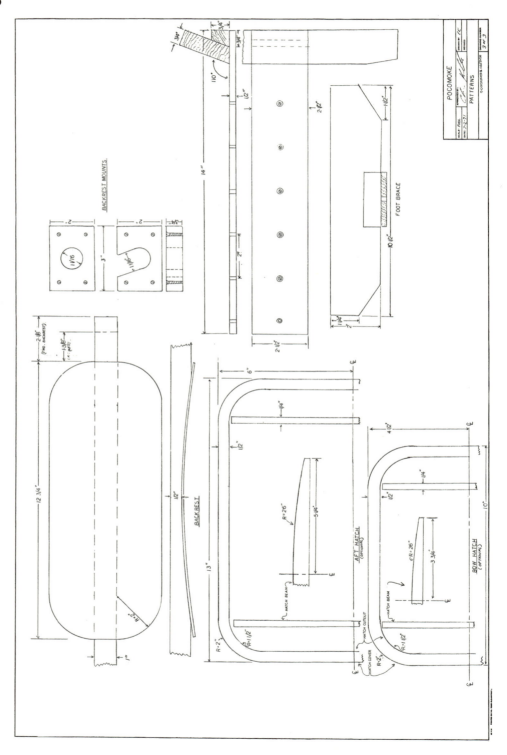

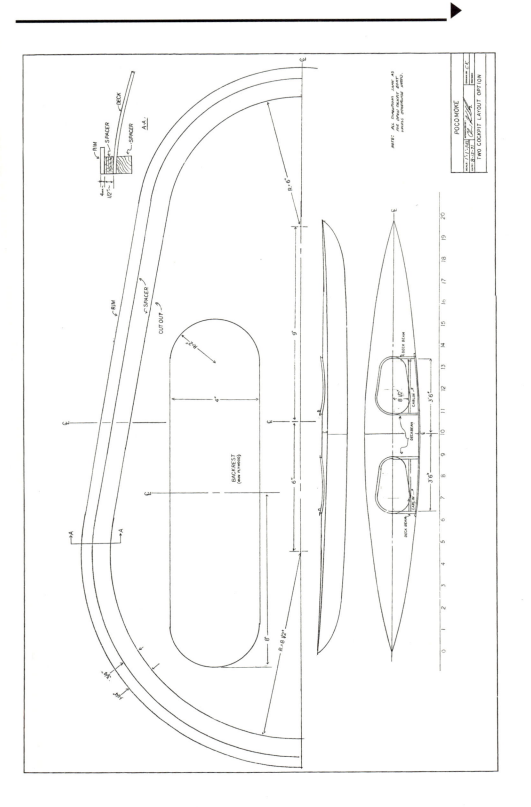

POCOMOKE

TWO COCKPIT LAYOUT OPTION

NOTE: ALL DIMENSIONS SAME AS
FOR OPEN DECKED BOAT
UNLESS OTHERWISE NOTED.

Chapter 6
Making the Hull Panels

B oats are composed of curves. For many woodworkers, this is a daunting fact. After all, you can't just slap down a straight-edge and draw a curve. But by using a few tricks, laying out the curved lines of the hull panels is not too difficult. When building a hard-chine boat, such as the Cape Charles, you can even get away with slight errors in your layout. On the other hand, compounded-plywood boats, such as the Yare and the Pocomoke, must have their panels laid out and cut exactly right if they are to "bend up" properly.

In building the Yare or the Pocomoke, all four hull panels will be cut from half a sheet of plywood, then joined with a scarf joint to form two long sections. It's easiest to lay out both panels on one half of the sheet first, then rip it in half, stack the two halves, and cut the panels out.

In building the Cape Charles, the plywood panels are joined with a scarf joint prior to drawing and cutting the panels out. I'll discuss layout first, then scarfing, so you'll need to reverse the order of these steps if you're building the Cape Charles.

Laying Out the Panels

Most kayak plans have layout diagrams showing the exact dimensions of the hull panels. Usually these include offsets from the edge of the plywood sheet or from a baseline. You'll have to transfer these measurements to your plywood sheet and then connect them with a curved or straight line.

Offsets are measurements at right angles to the baseline, centerline, or panel edge. They are points shown as a given distance along the baseline or centerline, then a given distance to the left or right of it.

Mark long baselines or centerlines on the plywood with a straight-edge or chalkline. If you don't have a sufficiently long straightedge, the factory-cut edge on another sheet of plywood works fine. When using a chalkline, first shake any excess chalk off the string as you pull it out of its case, otherwise it will splatter when snapped and leave a thick, imprecise line. Always measure from the edge of the chalkline rather than try to estimate its center; of course, you must always use the same edge of the chalkline.

Master boatbuilder
Yoachim Russ lays out
the panels for a kayak.
His batten is held in
place with clamps and
brads. Notice the long
straightedge that marks
the top of the panel.

Lay down your measurements with a rafter square to ensure that they are exactly at right angles to the baseline or edge. Mark each measurement point with a small, penciled cross. After you've laid out all the points, double-check them—it's less trouble than ordering more wood if you've goofed.

Use your straightedge to draw any straight lines on the panels, but the curved lines should be drawn with a *batten*. A batten is simply a thin, flexible strip of wood. Lengths of 1- x ¼-inch lath make good battens; ½-inch square spruce is even better. Select a piece that has extremely even grain and no knots. It should bend smoothly and evenly over its entire length. It's worth annoying your local lumberyard by looking through their entire stack for one good batten.

The batten is used like a flexible straightedge. Hold it against the measurement points as you draw the line. You can buy special lead weights, called ducks, to hold the batten in place, or you can drive small brads at each measurement point and hold the batten against these with clamps, a few bricks, or rocks. Take your time adjusting the batten to ensure a fair curve: that is, a curve without any bumps,

I use a batten to draw a fair curve. I have several battens of different thicknesses that are best for particular curves.

kinks, flat spots, or hollow areas. The only way I know to judge the fairness of a curve is to look down the batten. When you're satisfied that it is laying in a truly fair line, pencil in the curve.

Occasionally, you'll need to lay out a curve or arc by using its radius, which is given on the plan. A curve's radius is simply the distance from the center point of a circle to its perimeter. The best tool for laying out a radial curve is a set of trammels: these are a larger version of a bar compass used in drafting. The trammels are clamped to a wooden bar; one trammel holds a pencil, the other a sharp point. The trammels are adjusted to the proper distance apart and used like a compass. Of course, you can make longer bars and swing larger radii with trammels than with a compass.

If you don't have trammels, draw the curve by tying two small loops in a piece of string; the loops will hold a brad and a pencil at the same distance apart as the radius of the curve being drawn. Drive in the brad at the radius point, keep the string taut, and then swing the arc. Another method is to drill two holes in a strip of scrap wood, using one for the pencil and the other for the brad.

Cutting Out the Panels

Now that the hull panels are laid out and all the measurements dou-
ble-checked, it's time to cut them out. Fit your sabersaw with a fresh
10-tooth-per-inch woodcutting blade. The mirror-image port and
starboard sections should be cut from stacked panels to ensure that
they will be identical. Lay the plywood on your workbench with the
layout line just over the bench's edge. Clamp both panels together
so they won't shift as you cut.

Don't cut the panels exactly on the line. If you have a steady hand,
try to stay about ⅟₁₆ inch outside it; if not, aim for about ⅛ inch outside it. Later you'll trim the panels exactly to the line with a block
plane. Allow the sabersaw to find its best speed through the wood;
don't try to push it faster than it can cut. You may find it easier to
guide the saw with two hands. Always wear safety goggles so you
won't be temporarily blinded by a puff of sawdust. Keep moving the
panel on the workbench, so it's always supported an inch or so from
where you're cutting.

Trammels are a type of
compass used to draw
arcs or parts of a large
circle. In this case, the
arc forms the after end of
the kayak's hull panels.

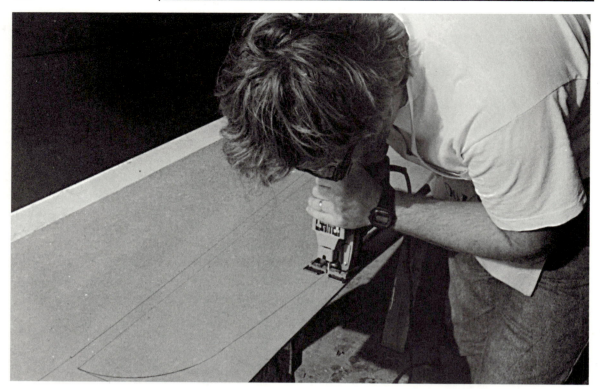

Hold the sabersaw with both hands and let it find its own speed. Cut just outside your layout line.

Planing the Panels

I prefer to remove the last bit of wood to the layout lines with a block plane instead of with a sabersaw because I'm much less likely to cut beyond the line with the plane. A plane also leaves a fairer curve and a smoother edge. It's important to keep the plane blade sharp and not set too deep. Though it might seem that planing is a tedious step, you can finish off the edges to a set of hull panels in about 20 minutes.

When trimming the cut-out parts, remember that the two sides of the boat must be absolutely, positively, and without doubt identical. If they aren't, the kayak will pull to one side, and you'll spend all your paddling time going in circles. With this in mind, support the panels so they don't droop over the edge of your workbench. Otherwise, the top panel will come out slightly larger than the bottom panel. Try to keep your plane perpendicular to the panels so as not to plane more from one than the other. Sight down the panels as you plane to make sure the edge is fair because it is easy to plane a flat spot. For this reason, it's better to plane to the outside of the pencil line. When you've finished planing, lay the panels on the shop floor and check once again that they're identical.

Scarf Joints

Kayaks are generally longer than sheets of plywood. So you'll need to join two or more pieces of plywood to form sheets a little longer than the kayak you intend to build. The best and most elegant way to accomplish this is with a scarf joint, which is two overlapping bevels glued together.

The idea behind a scarf is to provide a large surface for the glue to bond to. If the length of the joint is at least eight times the thickness of the wood, then a properly glued joint will be as strong as the wood. I've purposely broken numerous scarfed panels to see if the scarf was a weak point; in all instances the surrounding wood cracked first.

Cutting a Scarf Using a Block Plane

The simplest way to cut a scarf is with a block plane. Before you start be sure that the plane is sharp. Don't just feel it with your finger; try it out on a piece of plywood. The glue in plywood quickly dulls plane irons, so it might need to be resharpened after cutting a few scarfs. Set your blade for a shallow cut. This is better than planing off great

Use a block plane to trim the panels exactly to the layout lines. Plane the panels in pairs so they'll be identical.

◀

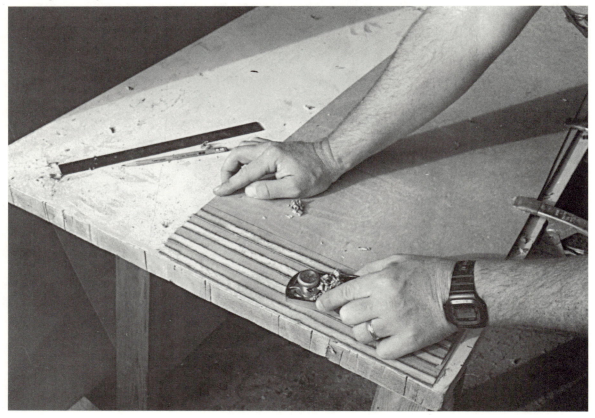

As you cut the scarf, the plywood's veneers will appear as bands. Notice how the four panels are stacked with their edges staggered.

swaths of wood all at once, because sooner or later you will tear out a big chunk and perhaps ruin the panel.

Before planing, the scarf joint has to be marked out. Begin by drawing a line along the joint's inside edge. Since you'll be cutting an 8:1 scarf this line will be one inch from the edge of the wood when joining 3mm plywood (3mm multiplied by 8 is 24mm, or about 1 inch). With 4mm plywood an 8:1 scarf would be 1¼ inches wide.

Line up the edge of the panel to be scarfed flush with the edge of your workbench. If the edge of the workbench is chewed up and scarred, tack down a good surface on it first. You will be removing the wood between the pencil line and the bottom edge of the panel where it meets the workbench. Start by holding the plane at a slight angle and slowly cut along the edge of the plywood. As a "ramp" is formed, the layers in the plywood will appear as bands. Try to keep these bands parallel as you plane. When you have a smooth, flat surface between your pencil line and a feather-like edge against the workbench you're done.

This scarf was cut with a belt sander. It needs to be touched up with a block plane.

To save time, you can cut scarfs on as many as four panels at once. Position the panels flush with the edge of the workbench. Slide the top panel back so that its edge rests on the pencil line of the panel below it; stagger all the panels that you're scarfing in this way and clamp them to the workbench. Now you can cut a ramp between the pencil line on the top sheet and the edge of the workbench, just as you would with a single sheet.

Cutting scarfs with a block plane is probably easier to do than to explain. Practice on a piece of scrap and you'll soon get the hang of it.

Other Ways to Cut Scarfs

Cutting scarfs with a block plane is simple and convenient. But professional boatbuilders, who must be very efficient to make a living, have come up with several time-saving methods for cutting scarfs. If you decide to build more than one kayak, one of these methods is worth trying.

I cut many of my scarfs with a belt sander. The technique is similar to using a block plane. Mark the edge of the scarf and stagger the panels at the edge of your bench. Sand away the wood to form a ramp instead of planing it off. Hold the sander so the belt runs down the ramp, not up or sideways to it. This will keep the plywood from tearing. It's easy to sand off too much wood, so work slowly. An 80-grit sanding belt seems best for cutting scarfs.

Another method I've used requires a router and jig. The router is fitted with a wide mortising bit and mounted on a short board. The board, with the attached router, slides up and down a frame, which is set at the proper angle to cut an 8:1 scarf. The frame, or jig, fits over the plywood panel to be scarfed, and you push the router along to cut a perfect scarf. The only drawback is that the set-up can take as long as cutting the scarf with a plane or belt sander. Of course, a production shop could dedicate a router and table exclusively to scarfing and have an almost perfect system.

I also own a scarfing attachment for my circular saw. It's made by West System and cuts scarfs on panels up to ⅜ inch thick. The attachment consists of a guide that holds the saw at the proper angle to the panel. The device rests against a straightedge that is clamped to the panel. Again, the main drawback is setup time, and it won't handle several panels at once.

Gluing Scarfs

Though I've never heard of one failing, you should always be extra careful when gluing scarf joints. Check that the temperature is within the epoxy manufacturer's specifications, that the resin and hardener are mixed to exactly the right ratio, and double-check that the panels are perfectly aligned.

First, lay the panels to be joined on a flat surface with a sheet of plastic under the scarf. Mix an ounce or two of epoxy and thicken it to the consistency of honey. Spread some epoxy on both bevels. Carefully position the bevels and check that the panel is straight by stretching a string beside it. Cover the joint with a second sheet of plastic.

Clamping a scarf joint can be tricky. With very narrow panels or solid-wood strips, ordinary C-clamps will do the job, but with wider scarfs you have to be more creative. The easiest method is to use staples: lay a strip of thin scrap plywood over the plastic-covered joint

Clamping the scarf by stapling it to the work surface is quick and easy. The piece of scrap plywood will be pulled up with all the staples when the epoxy has cured. The string line running alongside the panels is used to check alignment.

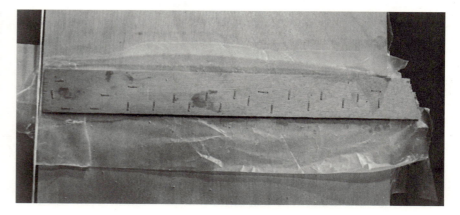

and drive a staple every inch or so along the joint. The staples must be long enough to pass through the scrap, the scarf, and into the surface they're resting on. (Hopefully it's not your hardwood floor.) Tap each staple with a hammer to ensure that it's fully driven. After the epoxy has cured, pull up the scrap strip and, with it, the staples. More than one panel can be stacked and glued this way, as long as the staples penetrate them. The tiny staple holes can later be filled with a mixture of epoxy and sawdust.

If you're a perfectionist, the idea of little staple holes in your boat may not appeal to you. In this case, clamp your panels by placing heavy weights on top of the joints. Full five-gallon buckets of water make good weights.

Most scarf joints will require a little sanding to remove the glue that's squeezed out of them. Sand the joint carefully so you don't cut through a layer of the plywood; 80-grit paper will work fine.

Commercially Scarfed Panels

Your plywood supplier may be able to scarf two or more panels for you. My supplier, Harbor Sales of Baltimore, Maryland, has produced a plywood sheet 50 feet long for a U.S. Naval Academy rowing barge. That was probably the longest sheet of plywood ever made in America. And they say they'll make a longer sheet if the customer can figure out how to get it home.

The author's shop? No, this is Harbor Sales in Baltimore, Maryland. Not only do they sell almost any type of marine plywood you may want, they will scarf it to whatever length you need. That door in the background opens, should you want a panel longer than the shop. (Photo courtesy Harbor Sales)

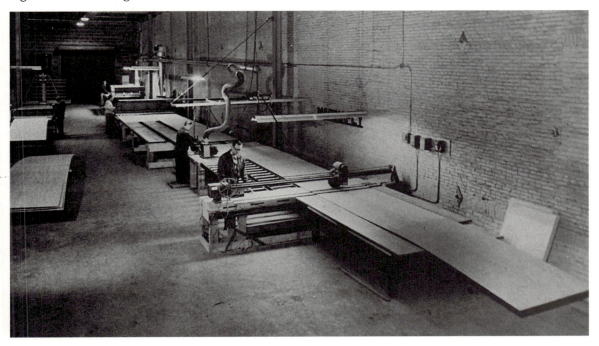

◀ ─────────────────────────────────

Harbor Sales's scarfed sheets are nicely done and inexpensive. But how do you economically ship a 16- or 20-foot-long panel? If you live near a supplier that can deliver scarfed panels or if you own or can borrow a truck, it might be worth considering commercially scarfed panels. But for most of us, the logistics of transporting them means we'll have to scarf our own.

Butt Joints

Some kayak plans call for butt joints instead of scarfs. Butt joints are simply two pieces of wood glued edge to edge, with a small piece of plywood or fiberglass tape glued under the joint for reinforcement. In addition to being rather inelegant and heavy, butt joints cause a flat spot when panels are bent. On relatively flat areas, such as decks, they are acceptable, but for hull panels I prefer to use a scarf.

Chapter 7
Assembling the Hull

There are several ways to assemble a plywood hull. One of the reasons I chose these three particular designs is that they are each assembled differently. So I've written the assembly sequences for the three boats separately. If you gain an understanding of how they go together, you'll be able to figure out most other designs with little trouble.

These three kayaks are built without hull forms and strongbacks. This will save you a lot of work because it takes about a day to construct the jigs. There is, however, the inevitable tradeoff: without a hull form and strongback, you must rely on your eye and skill to get the kayak's lines right. Of course, the shape of the panels will largely determine the hull configuration, but you must be sure that the hull does not bend, twist, or deform in some other way as it's being assembled. Not having a jig to hold the hull's shape is not as big a problem as it seems: if you periodically stand back and check the hull's lines as it is taking shape, you'll detect any problems that might be creeping in. Most folks have a better eye for symmetry and shape than they realize. Just don't forget to look.

Installing the Sheer Clamps

Before joining the hull, glue in the sheer clamps. I've tried gluing them into an assembled hull; trust me, it's easier this way. The sheer clamps are the two stringers that run along the joint between the side panels and the deck, which is called the *sheer*. They stiffen the kayak and provide the surface that the deck is glued and fastened to.

The sheer clamps are as long as the hull panels, which means that you'll probably need to scarf together two or more pieces of wood to obtain the correct length. The sheer clamps on all three boats are ¾ inch square, and can be ripped from a nominal 1-inch spruce or fir board. If you don't have a table saw, pay the lumberyard to cut them for you. At the same time, have some extra stock ripped for the seat risers and carlins (if you're building a Yare or Pocomoke).

Because these solid pieces are much thicker than plywood panels, the scarfs will be much wider; a scarf in a ¾-inch sheer clamp is 6 inches wide. You can cut scarfs in solid wood with a block plane, as

I use this simple sliding jig to cut scarfs for sheer clamps and rubbing strakes.

you did in plywood panels. But to save time, cut away most of the wood with a handsaw and finish up the ramp with your plane.

However, the easiest way to cut scarfs in solid wood is with a table saw. If you own or have access to a table saw, make a wooden jig that holds the wood at the proper angle to the blade. The jig will have to slide with the wood, so it should ride in the saw's miter-gauge groove. With the jig I made (see photo above), I can cut the scarfs needed for a set of sheer clamps in about 5 minutes. (A jig can also be built to use with a router or electric planer.) After gluing the scarfs, allow the epoxy to cure for 12 hours, then sand off any epoxy that's squeezed out of the joint.

Since the tops of the Cape Charles's side panels are flat, gluing on the sheer clamps is straightforward. But on the Yare and the Pocomoke, the sheer clamps follow a curve in the cockpit area. It's

When clamping the sheer-clamp scarfs, it's vital to check their alignment.

easiest to glue the sheer clamps onto both hull panels at once. That way, you can ensure that they are identically positioned, and you'll need only half as many clamps.

Start by stacking the panels back-to-back with the eventual outside faces turned in. Spread thickened epoxy along the entire length of both sheer clamps. Then, place them in the proper position on the hull and, every foot or so, clamp them together.

Clamp both sheer clamps to the plywood at once by laying the panels back-to-back.

At the cockpit area of the Yare and the Pocomoke, bend the sheer clamps to curve smoothly between the two straight sections. There will be two spots at either end of this area where the sheer clamps won't follow exactly the tops of the panels. At these points, the plywood will be planed off later. Wait overnight for the epoxy to cure before moving on to the next step.

Installing sheer clamps requires lots of clamps. If you don't own enough, borrow them from friends and neighbors or buy inexpensive 2-inch C-clamps.

Stitching and Taping

The stitch-and-tape assembly method solves the problem of trying to hold the hull panels into the shape of a kayak with conventional woodworking clamps. By tying the hull together with short lengths of copper wire, the large panels can be held in position while fiberglass tape and epoxy are applied to permanently join the seams. In the following section, I'll go over the basic stitching and taping techniques and then describe the exact sequence used to join the Yare's, Pocomoke's, and Cape Charles's hulls.

First, drill holes for the wire along the seam to be joined. They should be a little larger than the diameter of the wire used (about $\frac{1}{16}$ inch for 18-gauge wire). The holes should be about $\frac{1}{4}$ inch from the plank's edge and about 4 inches apart. It's best to stack, and then drill

Drill holes for the tie wires every 4 inches. Wire the panels together with short pieces of copper wire.

Twist the tie wires on the outside of the hull. Don't overtighten them or they will break or tear through the wood.

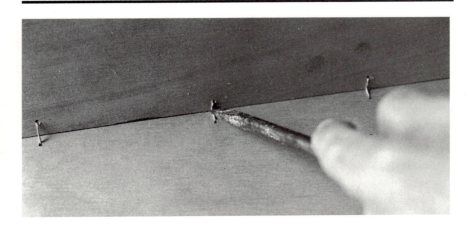

Push each wire flat against the inside seam with the point of a screwdriver. This tightens the wires and eliminates little bumps under the tape.

identical panels together, so the holes will be in matching positions.

Next, align and stitch the panels together. Cut wire into 3-inch lengths, pass the pieces through the holes, and twist the wires finger tight on the outside of the hull. Obviously, it's easier to do this with the hull upside down. When all the wire ties are in place and finger tight, tighten them further with a pair of pliers, but only until the panels touch.

Overtightening will pull the wire through the wood or break it. If some areas are difficult to pull together, drill a few more holes for additional ties. Pay careful attention to the curve of the seam; is it fair? If not, adjust the ties or remove them and touch up the panels with your plane. Finally, flip the hull over and, using a screwdriver point, push down each wire so it lies flat against the inside seam.

As you wire the boat's bow and stern together, you'll have to stop and cut a bevel in the sheer clamps, so they'll meet at a point. Make

The sheer clamps are beveled to meet in a point. This is a tricky step, so take your time. Notice the tie wire under the bow.

this tricky cut carefully with your handsaw. Cut the sheer clamps a little proud and then plane them until they fit perfectly. After you've wired the bow and stern together, check that the hull is symmetrical. If the panels are misaligned by even an ⅛ inch, the boat could pull to one side. Run a string line down the center of the hull, and use your square to check that both sides of the hull are equidistant from it. If the hull is twisted, push it into shape.

Start taping the seams by mixing some epoxy, thickening it to the consistency of caulk, and apply a bead of it on each seam. Smooth down the bead so it forms a fillet just covering the tie wires.

Epoxy manufacturers sell disposable syringes that make it easy to apply an even epoxy bead. Another neat way to apply a bead of epoxy is to cut the corner off a Ziploc-type plastic bag and push a small piece of plastic tube through it. Tape the tube into place and pour some thickened epoxy into the bag. Squeeze the bag to lay down a bead of epoxy on the seams.

Cut a piece of fiberglass tape to the required length, and lay it on the seam. Mix some more epoxy, but don't thicken it; brush it onto the tape, saturating it and the wood below. Apply another layer of tape and saturate it, likewise a third layer, if the building instructions call for it. It's best to stagger the tape, side to side, by a fraction of an inch so the edges don't line up and cause a hard spot. Also, stagger the ends by a couple of inches. Using a jabbing motion with your brush, work any air bubbles or dry spots out of the tape. Mix and brush on more epoxy as you need it, until the fiberglass is thoroughly saturated; it should be translucent with no opaque areas remaining.

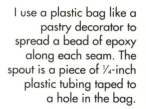

I use a plastic bag like a pastry decorator to spread a bead of epoxy along each seam. The spout is a piece of ¼-inch plastic tubing taped to a hole in the bag.

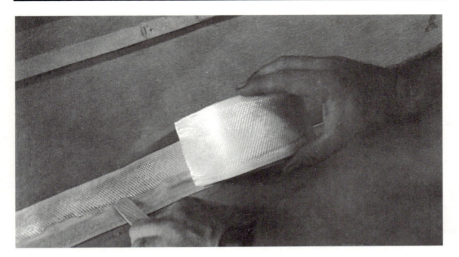

Lay the tape onto each seam; the bead of epoxy will hold it in place until you wet it out.

However, avoid brushing on more epoxy than required: it will add needless and expensive weight but little strength. If you plan to epoxy-saturate the hull's interior, you can do it now. Just brush two thin coats of epoxy onto all the exposed wood inside the hull; but don't coat the outside of the hull yet.

Once the epoxy has cured, gently turn the hull upside down and cut off the wire ties. Scrape or sand off any epoxy that's dripped through the seam. With a pair of side cutters, cut off the wires almost flush to the wood, so that only a minimal amount of sanding and planing will be required to smooth the joint. Remember that if you varnish your hull, this seam will be visible, so sand or plane it carefully.

Work all the air bubbles and dry spots out of the epoxy with a disposable brush. This is a good time to seal the inside of the hull.

When the epoxy inside the hull has cured, flip the boat over and cut off the wire ties. Then sand or plane the seams.

Use only unthickened epoxy on the outside of the boat. Lay the tape over the seam as before, then saturate it and work all the air bubbles out of the tape. Apply a second layer of tape, if required by the plans, and work the bubbles out of it. When the epoxy has started to harden, brush on one or two more coats to fill the tape's weave.

Tape the outside seams as you did the inside. A disposable bristle brush works better than the roller I'm using here.

Unlike paint and varnish, epoxy is best overcoated before it's fully hardened. The chemical bond between a fresh coating and a partially cured coat is very strong, so there's no need to sand between coats of epoxy, if less than 72 hours have elapsed since the previous coat was applied.

Occasionally, the tape won't lie flat on the hull. This often happens where it passes over sharp corners, such as at the bow and stern. One way to correct the problem is by draping plastic wrap over the wet tape and pushing it into the epoxy; the tape will be held down, and the plastic will peel off easily after the epoxy has hardened.

Joining the Hulls

In this section, I'll apply the stitch-and-tape method to our three boats. This is the only step where the techniques used to build the Yare, the Pocomoke, and the Cape Charles differ substantially. Follow these separate descriptions for joining the hull of the boat you're building.

Joining the Yare's Hull

The Yare's hull is probably the trickiest of the three to join. Since there are no keelson or chines to keep the hull rigid while it's being put together, the builder must "eyeball" the proper shape. And while it's being initially taped, the panels will have little resemblance to the final hull shape.

Start by drilling tie-wire holes along the keel line. Then lay the twin hull panels on your sawhorses; the

The two panels of a Yare's hull are ready to be wired together. They are clamped to a board under the scarf to help keep them aligned.

sheer clamps are up, and keel lines are touching at the scarf. The center eight feet of the two panels will be wired together and taped first. However, you'll notice that the panels don't touch over much of their length. But if you push down near the center of the panels, they'll bend into a shallow "U" and come together.

Wire the panels together for 4 feet to either side of the scarf. Twist the wires loosely on the outside of the boat while pushing the panels down. They must be almost flat across the scarf joint when they are taped. You can hold the panels in this alignment by sliding a scrap board under the scarf joint and clamping the sheer edges to it. Before clamping, place small spacers, about ¾ inch thick, between the sheer edges and the board. The spacers introduce a shallow V that adds rigidity to the boat. The ends of the panels, supported by the sawhorses, should now be considerably higher than the center part of the hull, which will droop down about 2 feet.

When stitched together, the ends of the panels must be higher than the middle. The weight of a full gallon-can of epoxy holds the panels in position so I can tighten the stitches.

Tighten the tie wires so the two panels touch along an 8-foot length. Then, with a screwdriver point, push the wires flat against the seam on the inside. It's particularly important with the Yare that the center seam runs in a smooth curve without any bumps, flat spots, or hollows. Even a slight imperfection will be greatly magnified when the hull is pulled together. Don't hesitate to cut your wire ties and touch up the panel edges with a plane or sandpaper if they aren't perfect. A few extra minutes spent getting this seam just right can save you extra work later on.

The center seam will initially be joined with three layers of fiberglass tape on the inside and one on the outside. Mix up a few ounces of thickened epoxy and spread a bead over the joint. It should just cover the tie wires and fill any gaps between the panels. Lay an 8-foot piece of fiberglass tape over the seam. Mix an additional 8 ounces of epoxy, but don't thicken it.

Saturate the tape with epoxy. Next, put down a 7½-foot length of tape over the first and saturate it. Finally, lay a 7-foot piece of tape over the first two and saturate it. After the epoxy has hardened, turn the boat over, cut off the wires, sand the seam, and, using the same procedure as before, apply 8 feet of tape along the outside joint. Allow the epoxy to cure overnight before proceeding.

Wire together the bow and stern sections of the boat; as you pull the hull together, it will start to assume its final shape. Cut the bow and stern bevels in the sheer clamps so they meet in a point. Pull the hull together until its maximum beam is 24 inches, and hold this measurement with pipe clamps or string. Use a string line and square to check that the hull is symmetrical.

Apply two layers of tape to the end sections of the hull seam, just as you did to the center section. These should overlap the center tape by a few inches. Use a thin piece of wood or a disposable brush to push the tape and epoxy into the narrow ends of the hull.

It is sometimes difficult to eliminate a seam bulge that forms where the center section's tape ends. If you can't squeeze the seam shut at this point, cut the original tape back along the seam for a few inches;

(left) The center 8 feet of the hull is taped first; then the boat is "rolled up" by wiring together the bow and stern sections.

(right) The ends of the hull are wired together and the inside tape is applied. Notice that the center piece of outside tape is also in place; it was applied prior to wiring the ends together.

a hacksaw blade is good for this job. Then add a few additional wire ties through the tape to pull the seam shut. Occasionally, a hull will have a concave "dip" along the seam. This is caused when the hull panels are planed too flat. This flaw can be corrected by slitting the taped seam along the affected area, pushing the panels out slightly, and retaping. You might need to jam a splinter of wood or wooden match stick into the seam to keep it in position while you retape it.

After the epoxy inside the boat has cured, turn the hull upside down, cut off the wire ties, and sand or scrape the epoxy that's dripped through the joint. Tape the outside seam from bow to stern with two lengths of tape. Remember to use only unthickened epoxy when taping the outside of the hull; brush on extra coats to fill the tape's weave completely.

A keelson installed in a Pocomoke should look like this one, installed in a Skua 16.

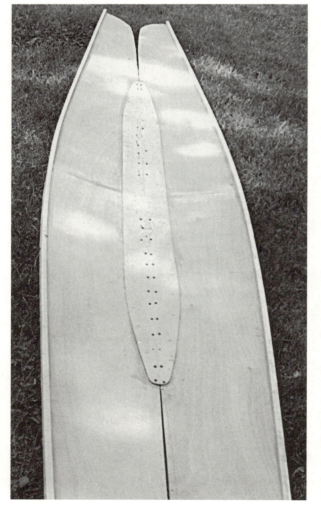

Joining the Pocomoke's Hull

The Pocomoke's hull is much like the Yare's; however, it has a keelson to which the two hull panels are glued and nailed, prior to taping the boat's ends. The keelson adds a little weight to the boat, but it also adds rigidity and eliminates hollows in the center seam.

The keelson is made from a ¾- x 2½-inch x 10-foot length of fir or spruce. Cut the taper in the keelson's ends as shown in the plans. Bevel its edges with a plane or round them with a router. Then draw a centerline down the bottom.

Mark the keelson's position on the two panels: it extends 5 feet to either side of the scarf's center. Drill wire-tie holes in the panels, from the point the keelson ends to the tips of the bow and stern.

Spread thickened epoxy along the bottom of the keelson, and then nail the panels to the keelson. Starting at the center of the keelson, drive a bronze ring nail every 3 inches and ½ inch in from the seam. Fasten both panels at once, alternately working at one end of the boat then the other; use the centerline you drew as a guide to keep the keelson centered.

You'll have to bend, or spring, the keelson as you work toward the ends; an assistant can be a great help in holding the keelson in this sprung position as you nail. After nailing the panels, turn the hull over and wipe up any epoxy that squeezed out from under the keelson. Wait for the epoxy to cure before going on.

Next wire the bow and stern together, twisting the wires on the outside of the hull. When the sheer clamps have been beveled to meet neatly at a point, pull the hull together so it's maximum beam is 27 inches. Apply a bead of epoxy, then a layer of tape to the hull seam, from the ends of the keelson to the bow and stern. The tape should overlap the keelson by an inch or two. Saturate the tape with unthickened epoxy; add another strip over the first and saturate it. You might also need a few extra wires to close up the seam near the ends of the keelson.

When the epoxy has hardened, turn the hull over, cut off the wire ties, and sand the seam. Next, apply two full-length strips of tape to the outside seam. Saturate each layer with unthickened epoxy and work out any bubbles or dry spots. Finally, fill the tape's weave with two more coats of epoxy.

This is not an injured whale; it's the bottom of my Pocomoke. Notice the pattern of ring nails holding the hull panels to the keelson. Once the nails are in place, this hull is built just like the Yare's hull.

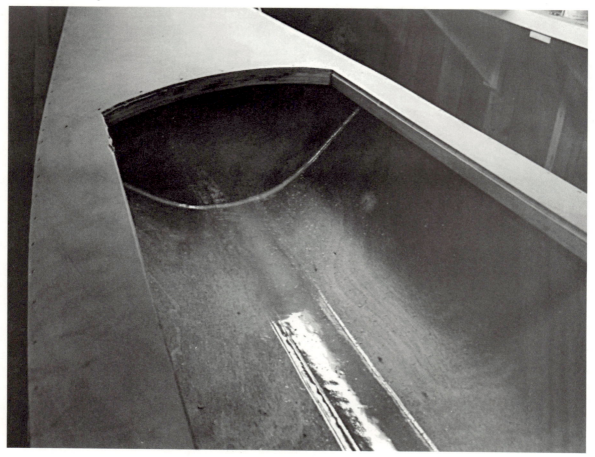

Yoachim Russ built his Pocomoke without a keelson. He did a fine job installing plywood bulkheads.

Joining the Cape Charles's Hull

Unlike the Yare and the Pocomoke, the Cape Charles's hull is made up of four panels. It might appear to be a harder hull to assemble, but it's actually very straightforward though more time consuming. First, the side panels are joined to each other at the bow and stern, and then the bottom panels are wired together along the keel line. Lastly, the bottom is wired to the sides and the seams are taped.

Begin by drilling tie holes along the bottom edge of the side panels and along the center edge of the bottom panels. Wire the ends of the side panels loosely together up to the point where the bottom panels will meet them (this point is shown on the plans). Spread the side panels apart so the maximum beam is about 25 inches; use a stick or board jammed between the sheer clamps to keep them apart. Cut bevels in the ends of the sheer clamps so the bow and stern meet at a point.

Now, wire the two bottom panels loosely together along the center seam with the wire twists on the outside of the hull. Lay the bottom panels on the overturned side panels. Drill tie holes along the outside edge of the bottom panels that correspond with the holes you drilled previously in the side panels. Wire the bottom panels to the side panels, again with the wires twisted on the outside of the hull.

The Cape Charles's maximum beam is located 9 feet 6 inches from the tip of the bow. At this point, use a spreader stick to make the kayak's maximum beam at the gunnel 25½ inches and with a second stick, push out the beam at the chine to 21 inches. If these measurements are correct the hull will assume its proper shape, except at the ends. Near the bow and stern, where all four panels meet, the bottom tends to flatten out. Use a clamp to squeeze them into a V shape; the angle should be as drawn in section A-A on page 1 of the plans.

The Cape Charles's two side panels are wired together first; then the bottom is wired to them. A spreader stick holds the sides to the proper beam measurement.

Three pieces of tape come together at the Cape Charles's bow and stern; it will take a little time to get this nice and smooth.

Check the seams for any bumps or hollows and adjust the ties to eliminate them. Now gently turn the hull over (rightside up). The hull must now be carefully supported, otherwise it will be distorted where it rests on the sawhorses or workbench. Push down the tie wires inside the hull and fill the seams with a bead of thickened epoxy. Apply a strip of tape to each of the three inside seams. Saturate the tape, apply second strips, and saturate them.

When the epoxy has hardened, turn the hull over and cut off all the wire ties. Sand or plane the seams, making them smooth and slightly rounded. Apply two layers of tape to each of the three outside seams, using only unthickened epoxy.

Finally, put your hull aside for 12 hours while the epoxy cures. Congratulate yourself: you've completed the hardest step in building your kayak.

Chapter 8
Installing the Deck

A kayak's deck is its most visible part; the deck is what you see when paddling and what others will see first when they look at your boat. You'll certainly want to varnish your deck to show off the wood, so try especially hard to do a neat, clean job of installing it. A minor flaw on the hull can always be hidden with a little fairing compound and a good paint job, but every scratch, dent, and tear in the deck shows.

But since you've already completed the hull, your woodworking skills are tuned up, and installing the deck will be easier for you than building the hull. Working on the deck is an exciting step: you'll finally have an idea of what the finished boat will look like. Even though there will still be a lot to do, it will all seem downhill once the deck is in place.

Before building the deck, you'll have to install the structure that gives it shape and support. This includes making and fitting the deck beams and carlins, and planing the tops of the sheer clamps. You may also want to install bulkheads and backing plates for a rudder before the hull is buttoned up.

The Deck Beams

The deck beams span the hull forward and aft of the cockpit. They support the deck and coaming, help hold the hull at the proper beam, and add rigidity to the kayak. The beams for our three kayaks are curved, or cambered, like the decks. They are made by laminating thin spruce or pine strips over a simple jig.

The radius of a beam describes its curvature: smaller means more curve and a higher deck; larger means less curve and a flatter deck. The radii of the deck beams for our three kayaks are shown on the plans. The Cape Charles and the Yare have 3mm plywood decks; the maximum radius I like to use for 3mm decks is 16 inches. Bending the deck to a radius smaller than this is difficult to do without causing the fasteners at the deck's edges to tear through the wood or the plywood to crack. For boats with a 4mm plywood deck, such as the Pocomoke, a deck radius of around 20 inches is the maximum I would attempt.

If you'd like to increase the volume of your kayak or gain extra knee room, there's no harm in decreasing the deck beam's radius slightly,

Use a simple jig, like this one, to make laminated deck beams. Wrap the deck beam in plastic, so it won't be glued to the jig.

though the appearance of the boat will change. My preference for single kayaks is an 18-inch radius forward and a 24-inch radius behind the cockpit. The transitional area between the two different deck cambers worries some builders. But given the flexibility of 3mm plywood, the deck panels blend together nicely. On doubles, decked with 4mm plywood, I find a 26-inch radius most pleasing to the eye. The camber of the deck does not have to be radial: you could draw it as a section of a parabola or a combination of two radii.

Making the Deck Beams

The deck beams for single kayaks should be about ¾-inch thick and for doubles about 1-inch thick. Lattice 1¼ x ¼ inches makes perfect stock for laminating deck beams, and it's readily available at lumberyards. Cut the lattice into strips a few inches longer than the deck beam. There are three strips for each ¾-inch-thick deck beam and four strips for 1-inch deck beams.

You can make a simple bending-jig, like the one shown in the photo at left, in just a few minutes. First, draw the required radius on a piece of scrap board; remember that if the radius shown on the plans is to the top of the deck beam, then you must subtract the thickness of the beam from it to find the radius of your jig. Next, cut the board along this line. Finally, drill large holes for the clamps an inch below the curved edge.

You can make another type of jig by drawing the radius line on a board and then screwing blocks of wood to the board, along the radius line. This device is a bit more trouble to make, but it's easier to keep the wood strips aligned on it. If you'll be building several boats, it's worth the extra effort.

Lay the strips of lattice on a piece of plastic and spread thickened epoxy on the surfaces to be joined. Stack the strips and wrap them in the plastic and they won't stick to the jig. Clamp the strips onto the jig as shown in the photo above and allow the epoxy to cure overnight.

If you plan to build several kayaks, I suggest you make this improved deck beam jig. This deck beam will be used in a Pocomoke.

Installing the Deck Beams

When the clamps are removed from the jig, don't be concerned if the deck beam springs back a little; that's normal. Scrape off epoxy that's squeezed out from between the strips, then sand and plane the edges of the deck beams. With the hull clamped open to the proper width, mark the position of the deck beams on the sheer clamps. Hold the deck beams where they will be fastened on the sheer clamps and mark their lengths. Cut the deck beams to length carefully; this is another of those tricky bevels. I prefer to cut them a bit long and then trim them for a perfect fit.

Glue the deck beams into place at the positions you marked. It's convenient, though not essential, to fasten the beams into place with long, thin screws that pass through the sheer clamps. Predrill the holes for these screws, so they won't crack the sheer clamps. If you're concerned with saving a few ounces of weight, remove the screws after the epoxy cures, or leave them out altogether and simply clamp the deck beams into place until the epoxy cures.

Installing the Carlins

Carlins are essentially deck beams that run fore and aft. They run between the deck beams at the edge of the cockpit cutout. They strengthen the area around the cockpit and provide a gluing surface for the coaming. The carlins in both the Yare and the Pocomoke are made from the same ¾-inch stock used for the sheer clamps.

Glue the carlins into place so that their top edges are level and their sides vertical. You can hold them in place while the glue sets up, with clamps, or with long, thin screws through the deck beams. Don't

With the deck beams and carlins installed, this hull awaits its deck.

be too concerned with getting a perfect joint here, or for that matter with the joint between the deck beam and sheer clamp; the deck itself reinforces these joints. After the epoxy has cured, plane the tops of the carlins to follow the curve of the deck beams.

Planing the Sheer Clamps

The angle between the deck and hull of a kayak is not a perfect 90 degrees, but the corners of the sheer clamps are. So the top edges of the sheer clamps need to be planed to allow the deck to follow a smooth curve, from gunnel to gunnel.

You could do this by eye, but by using a template with the same curve as the underside of the deck, you can see exactly how much wood needs to be planed off. The radius of the underside of the deck is, of course, the same as the top of the deck beams. Make your template by tracing the deck beam's radius onto a piece of cardboard or scrap plywood and cutting it out. Hold the template across the hull on the sheer clamps; you'll be able to judge exactly how much wood has to be removed. Plane the sheer clamps until they follow the curve of your template. If you have deck beams of different radii, you'll need two templates. The short sections of sheer clamp between the deck beams can be planed easily by eye.

Cutting Out the Deck

If you studied the plans in Chapter 5, you may have wondered if I'd forgotten to give dimensions for the kayaks' decks. I left them off because it's easier to use a completed kayak hull as a template to mark the deck's shape.

Both the forward and after deck sections are cut from a single sheet of plywood, so you'll have to draw them on the sheet. Place the plywood on your hull and bend the panels over the deck beam. Unless you're a professional wrestler, trying to hold the plywood down while drawing on its underside is almost impossible. Recruit a helper to hold the plywood down while you trace the hull shape onto it. Do this for both the forward and after deck sections. Since you'll have to bend the deck down again while attaching it, ask your helper to return soon.

Some longer boats, like the Cape Charles, require a third section of deck scarfed onto the bow. Mark the shape of this, leaving enough extra for the scarf joint, but don't attach it until after you've cut the main sections out.

The deck sections should be about ½ inch larger than your scribe lines indicate. If you're building the Cape Charles, or another long kayak, scarf the extension onto the foredeck; this extension should also be oversized. When possible, fit the deck panels so they meet at the widest part of the cockpit; this way the joints will be as short as possible.

It's best to seal the deck's underside and, if you haven't done it yet, the inside of the hull before installing the deck. The alternative is to crawl into the bow and stern later. You could use paint or varnish to seal the hull and deck, but I prefer epoxy resin applied with a foam roller. Use half of a 9-inch roller on a half-width roller (available at paint stores); it's easier to maneuver than a full-size roller, and it's less expensive. Two coats of epoxy provide an adequate seal.

Fastening Down the Deck

Before fastening down the deck, give one last thought to anything you might want to install inside the hull while it's still open. Bulkheads could be built later, but it's easier to fit them now. If you install a rudder, will it have a mount held on with screws? If so, you will need to glue backing plates into the stern now; read Chapter 10 before fastening down the deck if you plan to install a rudder.

The deck and hull will be held together primarily by the epoxy resin in the hull-to-deck joint. But until the epoxy cures, the plywood must be mechanically joined or clamped. The stitch-and-tape

Use a foam roller to seal the underside of the deck panels with epoxy. This is half of a 9-inch roller, used with a narrow roller frame.

method could be used to hold them together, but you would have to drill through the sheer clamps. An easier way is to drive ring nails, screws, or staples into the sheer clamps. Of these fasteners, I'm most satisfied with ring nails. Bronze ¾-inch 14-gauge ring nails have excellent holding power and very thin heads that can be driven flush with the plywood deck. They're easy to use and make a nice pattern on a bright-finished deck. I can live with the few extra ounces of weight the nails add.

The problem with screws is that the heads of most are so thick they will completely penetrate the thin deck, therefore providing marginal holding power. A solution is to use flat-head screws but remove them after the epoxy cures. The holes they leave must be filled before finishing. Using temporary screws is probably only worth the trouble if you're striving to save every possible ounce of weight.

If the deck is stapled to the sheer clamp, the staples should be at least ½ inch long, or they'll pop out as you bend the deck. A combination of screws and staples—a screw every foot and staples in between—works nicely. Be sure the staples are stainless steel, Monel, or bronze. If you choose to use screws or staples the gunwales have to be painted to hide the holes, but most kayaks look nice with a paint stripe accenting the sheerline.

Start installing the deck by spreading thickened epoxy on top of the sheer clamps, deck beams, and carlins. Position one of the deck panels on the hull. Be sure that the deck rests firmly on the deck beam before starting to fasten it into place. Begin fastening at the center of the

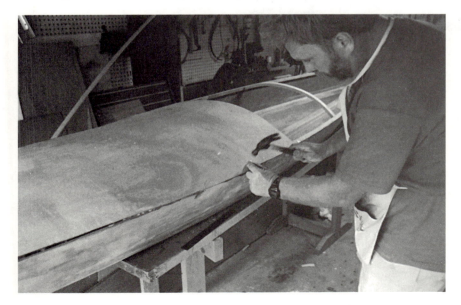

Bronze ring nails are the best fasteners for holding down the deck. Remember to alternate sides as you fasten down the deck.

Let the epoxy cure overnight before cutting the cockpit opening.

kayak and work toward the end, alternating between the port and starboard sides. If you were to fasten all of one side and then switch to the other, you'd end up with a lopsided curve in the deck.

After the first deck section is fastened down, lay the second section on the hull; it must butt tightly against the first section. There's no need to scarf the two main deck sections; a butt plate under this joint will reinforce it. If the two deck sections don't meet squarely, it's necessary to trim the edge of the second panel with your plane for a tight fit. When you're satisfied with the joint, fasten down the second deck panel exactly as you did the first.

After the epoxy in the hull-to-deck joint has hardened, cut off the excess deck with a sabersaw. Finish up by trimming it flush to the hull with a block plane.

Finishing the Hull-to-Deck Joint

The hull-to-deck joint, glued and nailed, is quite strong, and for most purposes there's no reason to reinforce it further. But if you paddle hard in difficult conditions, or if you abuse the boat, the seams should be taped with fiberglass.

If the joint is to be taped, first round it over with your block plane and sandpaper. (As you probably learned when taping the hull seam, it's hard to get tape to lay flat over sharp corners.) Tape this joint the same way you taped the outside hull joint: lay the tape on the joint, saturate it, work out the bubbles, and then apply more epoxy until the cloth's pattern is filled.

A kayak's hull-to-deck joint can take quite a beating, particularly when the boat is being transported. Adding a solid wood rubrail protects this joint and is an attractive trim piece. But I've found that the rubrail serves an equally valuable purpose. When paddling in a chop, the rail deflects water that would otherwise "climb" on deck and so makes for a drier ride.

Ash, teak, or white oak make pretty, if slightly heavy, rubrails. Select a piece with straight grain and rip, or have it ripped, into ¼- x ¾-inch strips. Shorter pieces can be joined into full-length strips with scarf joints. Spread thickened epoxy on the strip and tack it into place with ¾-inch brass brads, one every 4 inches or so. You can cut a bevel at the bow and stern and have the strakes meet at a point, but it's easier and more practical to cut them off flush with the boat's ends.

Other Types of Decks

Some kayak designs call for flat decks made from flat sections of plywood. Usually the forward deck is peaked. There may be a flat section at the bow and two sections forming the peak just forward of the cockpit, or the entire foredeck can be composed of two triangular pieces that meet in the center. These pieces are usually stitched and taped together.

The after deck may also be peaked, but it is usually a single flat sheet. The only real advantage of a flat rear deck is that you don't need a helper to install one.

The forward deck beam or beams, if any, can be made from two straight sections joined at the center with a lap joint. If the after deck is flat, the deck beams are simply straight.

Occasionally, you'll see a cloth deck on a plywood hull. These are usually made of aircraft Dacron, or canvas stretched over a framework of thin wooden members attached to the sheer clamps. Cloth decks can be very pretty and light. But they are more work to install than plywood decks. If you decide to install one read George Putz's excellent book, *Wood and Canvas Kayak Building* (International Marine, 1990).

Cutting the Cockpit Opening

Though some builders prefer to cut the cockpit opening prior to installing the deck, I think it's easier to do after the deck is in place. Plus, it gives your friends a chance to ask if you're building a submarine. The cockpit openings of these three boats are all differently shaped, but they are laid out and cut out in the same manner.

I like to have a paper or cardboard template of the cockpit opening that I can move around until placement of the opening is exactly right. To make a template, carefully draw the opening, as shown on the plan, on a large sheet of paper and cut it out with a pair of scis-

Use a paper pattern to lay out the cockpit opening. Though you can't see the lines in this photo, I've lightly marked the boat's centerlines to ensure that the cockpit will be in its proper position.

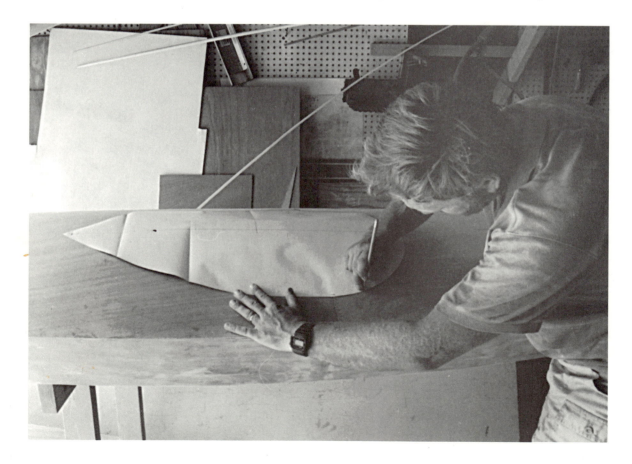

sors. Fold the template down its center line to check that it's symmetrical. If the plans you're using include a full-size drawing of the cockpit opening, you can simply cut it out to use as a template.

Cut a small hole in the deck, about in the center of where the cockpit will be. Insert your tape measure through this hole and measure from the hole to the deck beams and carlins; mark their location on the deck. Position the cockpit template on the deck and center it between the deck beams and the carlins. Mark the opening on the plywood and cut it out with your sabersaw.

After you've cut the cockpit opening, glue butt plates under the deck joint. These are simply little rectangles cut from scrap plywood that span the joint to reinforce it. They should be about two inches long and as wide as the distance between the sheer clamp and the cockpit opening or carlin.

Finally, stand back and admire your boat.

A butt plate reinforces the joint between the two deck panels.

Chapter 9
The Coaming, Seat, and Footbraces

Adding the coaming, seat, and footbraces finally turns your hull and deck into a kayak. Give these parts the attention they deserve because they directly affect your comfort. Seats, footbraces, and, in some cases, coamings, are not structural parts of the kayak, so you can modify them, design your own, or substitute commercially made versions.

Coamings

In addition to being functional, the coaming can be an eye-catching feature. You can make a simple but strong flat plywood coaming, or you can show off your joinery skills with a solid wood or bent-wood coaming.

The size of the coaming is important: if its opening doesn't fit a spray skirt that you can buy, you'll have to make one. The right size coaming will also allow you to raise your knees while sitting in the kayak yet enable you to brace them under the deck.

I'll describe how to make the two types of coamings shown on the plans for our three boats plus another coaming that can be adapted to many kayaks.

Making a Flat Laminated Coaming

The coamings for the Yare, the Cape Charles, and the two-cockpit version of the Pocomoke designs are made by laminating a ring of ¼-inch plywood onto a spacer that's glued to the kayak's deck. This is the most common type of coaming on wooden kayaks. It's popular because it's strong and easy to make. The coamings shown on the plans will accommodate many popular brands of spray skirts; you could, however, easily change the dimensions to accommodate odd-size skirts or odd-size paddlers.

The first step in making a flat, laminated coaming is cutting the spacer the rim will be glued to. Make the spacer from ½-inch plywood, which can be exterior grade since it's barely visible and is sealed with epoxy. The spacer can also be made from two layers of the ¼-inch plywood that was used for the rim, or from four layers of left-over

3mm plywood. It's more economical to cut the spacer in two pieces and lay out the two pieces so they "nest." This way you'll avoid ending up with a large useless piece of wood, cut out of the center of a one-piece spacer.

The coaming's top ring or rim should be made from ¼-inch plywood. I usually use lauan. Marine-grade lauan looks a bit better than exterior grade, but both hold up well. Of course, you could use any waterproof ¼-inch plywood, or even solid wood; how about a zebra wood coaming rim? If you tend to abuse your kayaks, laminate on a second ring or sheath the rim with fiberglass cloth to increase its strength.

After the spacer and rim are ready, spread thickened epoxy on both sides of the spacer and position it on your kayak. Next, set the rim on top of the spacer. Clamp the pieces into place after inserting pads of scrap plywood between the clamps and the rim. This keeps the wood from being dented. Wipe up any epoxy that's squeezed out under the rim; otherwise, the spray skirt will catch on gobs of hard epoxy.

Once the epoxy has cured, sand the inside of the cockpit opening. If you weren't precise when you cut the pieces, there will be lots

The Yare and Cape Charles's coamings are laminated from rings of plywood. The top ¼-inch-thick ring is a little wider than the bottom ½-inch-thick ring, thus forming a lip for a spray skirt.

of sanding before the inside is smooth and even; a rasp or belt sander will knock down the really rough sections. When you're finished, the inside of the opening should show a handsome pattern of plywood layers. Brush a coat of unthickened epoxy onto the exposed edges of plywood around the coaming; after it's soaked in, brush on a second coat.

Making the Pocomoke's Coaming

When drawing the plans for the Pocomoke, I was aware that this type of boat would usually be paddled without a spray skirt. Since I was planning to use it as a platform to take nature photographs, I designed it with a large open cockpit. I also knew from paddling other doubles that the occasional motorboat wake or rogue wave would wash it's deck, so I designed a coaming that's higher than the one on my Klepper to better deflect boarding waves. The coaming has a small overhanging rim for a custom-sewn spray skirt when conditions get rough. This rim is also effective in deflecting water that washes up the coaming.

The spruce coaming on the Pocomoke is functional and handsome. But it's harder to make than a plywood coaming and can crack.

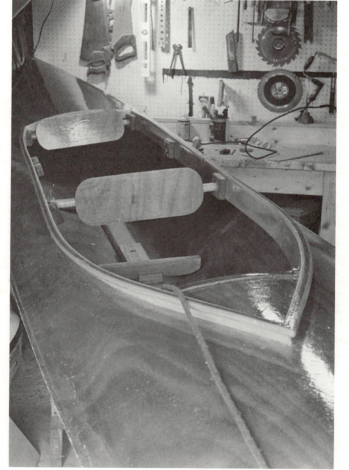

The Pocomoke's coaming can be made from $3/8$-inch solid wood, such as spruce or mahogany, or from $1/4$-inch plywood. For solid wood, you'll need to rip it to $3/8$-inch-thick stock or have your lumberyard run it through a thickness planer.

Cut the wood into two $2^{1}/_{2}$-inch strips, then lay out and cut the notch at the coaming's forward end as shown in the plans. Before trimming the coaming's after end, trial fit it to ensure a tight fit. Cut out the banana-shaped third piece of the coaming, which fits at the cockpit's after end, with your sabersaw. Check that everything fits; when you're satisfied, glue the coaming to the carlins and deck. It will take quite a few clamps to hold the wood in place. The forward tip of the coaming can be tricky to join, and you'll need to cut another bevel there.

The small mahogany knees, the trim strip above them, and the mahogany strip in the coaming lip are examples of how you can dress up a wooden kayak without adding much weight.

Finally, try a bit of creative clamping to hold everything in position. Don't be stingy with the epoxy; run a good solid fillet at the coaming-to-deck joint, particularly on the underside. Glue the back section of the coaming to the deck over the after deck beam.

The coaming rim is made from two thin strips of wood that are glued to its top outside edge. These strips are ¼- x ⅜-inch solid wood. If the coaming is made of light-colored wood, consider using a dark (mahogany) strip next to it then a light (ash or pine) strip over that; the contrasting bands will be very pleasing. You could also use a piece of half-round molding from the lumberyard for the outside strip, giving it a smooth finished look. When gluing on the strips, use pads between the clamps and the wood, and be careful not to overtighten the clamps and dent the strips. Carefully cut a bevel where the strips meet at the bow and then sand down the point so it's not too long and sharp.

The two strips that make up the rim on the back section of the coaming must be bent across their wide dimension. If they're hard to bend, soak them in a tub of hot water for 30 minutes first. Clamp them into position but don't glue them to the coaming until they're dry.

When the epoxy has cured, plane and sand the edges of the coaming. The two after backrest brackets will serve as knees to reinforce the joint between the side- and back-coaming sections. But you may also want to add two small knees to reinforce the area where the coaming meets the forward deck beam, and to hide the gap that often forms here. Make these from some scraps of solid wood and glue them into place as shown in the photo on page 101.

I've seen coamings similar to these on single kayaks. But it's difficult to bend solid wood around a short single cockpit without using steam, and so they tend to end up being triangular in shape, which is not attractive. The bent plywood coaming described next might be a better solution.

Making a Bent Plywood Coaming

Over the years, I've fooled around with steam-bent coamings; eventually I concluded that they were too much trouble to make. In searching for an alternative, I designed a 3mm-plywood bent coaming that looks much like a steam-bent version. It was incorporated into a kayak, the Severn, that I designed for an article in *Fine Woodworking* magazine. This coaming is similar in many ways to the Pocomoke's coaming, and, like that coaming, it will keep the paddler fairly dry without a spray skirt. The disadvantage of this design is that it's not as strong as the flat, laminated coaming.

The Severn's coaming is made from a single 3¼-inch-wide strip of 3mm okoume plywood, bent around the perimeter of a teardrop-

The Severn-type bent plywood coaming is not unlike the Pocomoke's.

shaped cockpit. The coaming is glued to the deck beams, carlins, and deck, and is reinforced with a fillet of epoxy under the deck. Start by cutting the coaming and bending it into place inside the cockpit opening. Cut a notch in the forward ends so they will fit over the deck. Glue the okoume to the carlins and deck beams. A few strips of scrap wood wedged across the cockpit and some clamps at the carlins and deck beams will hold the coaming tight against the deck until the epoxy cures. Apply a fillet of epoxy and some short pieces of fiberglass tape along the deck's underside to reinforce it.

The cockpit rim is made of two thin strips of wood glued to the coaming's top edge, as on the Pocomoke. The strips should be ¼- x ⅜-inch ash or another easily bent wood. Glue them into place and bevel the ends where they meet.

When I first built this coaming, I was not sure how strong it would be and considered laminating a second layer of plywood inside the first. But the 3mm-thick coaming has held up well. You could also apply a layer of fiberglass tape to the inside and outside of the coaming to increase it's strength. An interesting variation of this coaming might be to make it round or oval as on a traditional Eskimo kayak.

Another of those tricky bevels is required at the severn-type coaming's "nose."

Seats

It's difficult to design simple wooden seats and backrests that are comfortable. I get one or two letters every year saying that I should stick to designing kayak hulls and hire someone else to draw the seats. In fact, many wooden-kayak builders prefer to use commercially made plastic or fiberglass seat units. I, however, have always favored simple plywood seats and backrests generously padded with closed-cell foam. Foam is the secret: no one over the age of 20 can sit on an unpadded kayak seat for long.

My Cape Charles's seat was held in place with this arrangement of shop scraps while the epoxy cured.

The wooden seats shown on the Yare and Cape Charles plans are cut from a piece of 3 or 4mm plywood. Cut the seat to the pattern shown on the plans, or cut a 12- x 14-inch rectangle and round its corners. Two seat risers are made from the same ¾- x ¾-inch stock used for the sheer clamps and the carlins; they keep the seat above any bilge water. Glue the seat risers to the hull and the seat to the seat risers. Be sure to seal the seat risers and the underside of the seat with epoxy prior to installing them. The seat should curve slightly to form a depression for your backside.

The seats for the Pocomoke are 4mm plywood that are screwed and glued to the keelson; use the pieces you cut out from the cockpit. If you plan to paddle the Pocomoke alone, it should accommodate a third, or center, paddling position consisting of a removable seat, backrest, and footbraces. The other two seats, backrests, and footbraces could also be removable to save weight. The easiest way to install removable seats is to use threaded brass inserts that are glued into holes drilled in the keelson. The seats are screwed or bolted into the inserts. Threaded inserts are available from larger hardware sup-

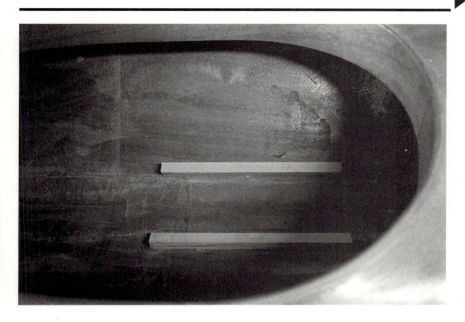

Two small cleats keep
the seat above the
bilge water.

pliers or cabinetmakers' supply houses. If you can't find brass inserts,
use the plastic variety made for screwing into sheet rock and plaster.

Backrests

Unless you plan to use a one-piece fiberglass or plastic seat, you'll
need to install a backrest. The simplest backrests are the commercially
made nylon and foam backbands used in whitewater kayaks; they are
easy to install and inexpensive. I prefer to make my own; a small oval
of plywood padded with closed-cell foam is a perfectly adequate backrest.

The Yare's backrest is made by gluing this oval piece of plywood
to the back edge of the coaming and to the after deck beam. Take
the time to sand the back of the coaming so the backrest isn't perfectly vertical; it'll be much more comfortable. You might sit in the
boat while a friend holds the plywood oval at various angles to determine which angle is most comfortable.

The Cape Charles' backrest is made by laminating a plywood oval
onto two pieces of lattice. This is the same method you used to laminate the deck beams. In fact, the 18-inch-radius jig you made for
the forward deck beam also works as a jig for the backrest. After laminating the plywood oval to the lattice, seal it with epoxy and varnish
it. The oval is then attached to the kayak's sheer clamps with a length
of 1-inch nylon webbing, as shown in the photograph on page 107.
Attach the webbing to the sheer clamps and backrest with ¾-inch

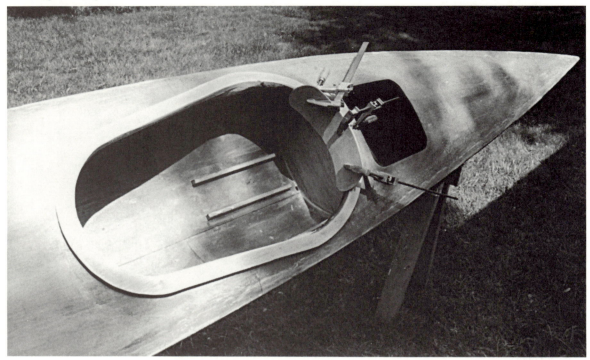

The simplest backrest is a piece of plywood glued to the back of the coaming. Be sure the angle of the backrest is comfortable before you glue it into place.

screws and finish washers. The webbing should be attached to the sheer clamps about 18 inches forward of the backrest. By adding a pair of adjustable plastic buckles, you can vary the position of the backrest. A second shorter length of nylon webbing is attached to the backrest and to the after deck beam to hold the backrest up. An adjustable buckle fitted on this piece allows the backrest to be raised or lowered.

The Pocomoke's backrest is also a plywood oval, but it is glued to a dowel that fits in mounts that are screwed and glued to the coaming. The dowels rotate in the mounts so the angle of the backrest conforms to the paddler.

Each pair of mounts consists of one that's simply a hole drilled in a block of wood into which the dowel fits, and another that has a U-shaped slot cut into the block. The backrest can be removed by lifting it out of the U-shaped mount. Patterns for the mounts are on the Pocomoke plans.

Cut the mounts with your sabersaw from ¾-inch-thick solid wood. Attach them to the coaming, in the positions shown on the plans, with epoxy and four 1-inch wood screws; be sure to predrill the screw holes.

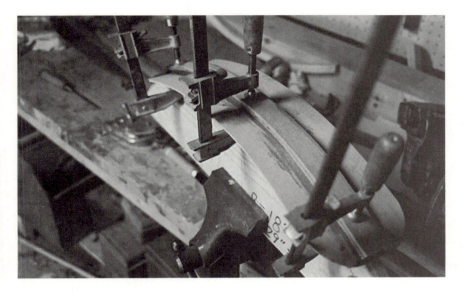

The Cape Charles's backrest is laminated on the same jig used to make the forward deck beam.

These nylon straps adjust the position of the Cape Charles's backrest.

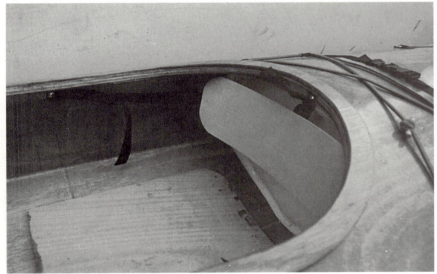

The after backrest mounts are also glued to the back coaming section for reinforcement. Bevel the back edges of these after mounts and they will fit neatly into the corners. A third set of mounts can be fitted for a center paddling position.

The dowel supporting the backrest can be ¾-inch hardwood from your lumberyard or an old broomstick. The backrest is glued into a scooped-out section on the dowel as shown on the plans. You can carve out this area with a block plane, knife blade, and sandpaper. If you use a spokeshave or draw knife, it will take less time.

The Pocomoke's backrests are glued to dowels that rotate in mounts screwed to the coaming. This after mount also serves as a knee, reinforcing the back section of the coaming.

Footbraces

Strong and properly positioned footbraces are essential to efficient paddling. Kayaks with rudders must have footbraces that slide or pivot to control the rudder. If more than one person will paddle the kayak, it should be fitted with adjustable footbraces.

My rather odd method of arriving at the proper position for footbraces is as follows: I tape the footbrace to my shoe and sit in the kayak; when satisfied that my feet are in the optimal position, I ask my assistant to reach into the kayak and mark the location. Try this method; just don't climb out of the boat and run for the phone in mid-fitting.

A nonadjustable footbrace can be made by simply gluing a block of wood inside your boat. A slightly more sophisticated version is shown on the plans for the Yare; these footbraces are cut from ¾-inch-thick solid wood and then glued and screwed to backing plates. Footbraces are subject to considerable loads, which must be distributed by backing plates installed under the footbraces. The backing plates are

This is a simple adjustable footbrace you can make and install in a Pocomoke or other kayak with a keelson.

rectangles of 3mm or 4mm plywood that are a couple of inches wider and longer than the footbrace.

The Pocomoke plans show a wooden adjustable footbrace system suitable for kayaks with keelsons. They are made from three solid-wood parts glued together. The footbrace is adjusted by moving screws that fit into the same type of threaded inserts that were used for the removable seats. Since a screwdriver or wrench is needed for adjustments these footbraces are not as convenient to adjust as commercially made models, but they are inexpensive and easy to make.

I've installed commercially made adjustable footbraces in most of the kayaks I've built because they work better than any that I can easily make. The aluminum and plastic Yakima footbraces favored by whitewater kayakers are probably the strongest and best made on the market. If you don't intend to install a rudder, they should be your first choice. The all-plastic Keeper footbraces, used in Aquaterra kayaks, are also well made, and they have the added advantage of being convertible to sliding peddles, should you later decide to fit a rudder.

Commercially made footbraces should, like homemade footbraces, be installed on backing plates glued to the inside of your hull. Most commercially made footbraces have aluminum rails that are difficult

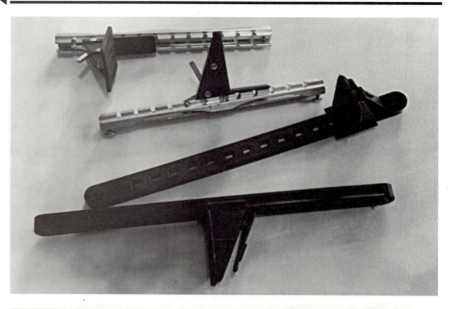

Commercial footbraces work better than any you can easily make. The top braces are made by Yakima and are popular with whitewater paddlers because of their strength; the bottom set are Aquaterra's keeper footbraces. They can be converted to control peddles if you later decide to install a rudder.

Footbraces should be mounted on backing pads to distribute the loads they are subjected to.

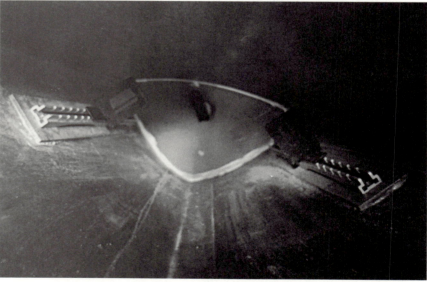

to glue properly. The surface of aluminum oxidizes quickly when exposed to air, but the bond between aluminum and epoxy is stronger if that surface is not oxidized. A way to increase the bond strength is to spread a little epoxy on the aluminum surface then wet-sand it. The epoxy will prevent air from reaching the freshly sanded surface. While the epoxy is still wet, screw the rail into place; be careful that you don't get any epoxy in the adjustment mechanism. I've recently tried gluing in footbraces with 3M 5200 sealant; they've held so far.

Chapter 10
Installing Bulkheads, Hatches, and a Rudder

I f you paddle in rough water, on windy days, on long trips, or you load your kayak up with camping gear, you'll probably want to install hatches, bulkheads, and a rudder in your new kayak. If, on the other hand, you do most of your paddling on calm, protected waters there's little point in complicating your simple craft. In either case, you can always add hatches, bulkheads, or a rudder later, if you decide you need them.

Bulkheads

Bulkheads limit the amount of water that can enter a capsized kayak, provide reasonably dry storage compartments, and add buoyancy to the kayak.

I now use 3-inch-thick closed-cell foam, rather than plywood, for

Using 3-inch closed-cell foam makes installing bulkheads easy. These slabs of foam also provide extra flotation. They can be cut with a long sabersaw blade, as seen here, or with a serrated kitchen knife.

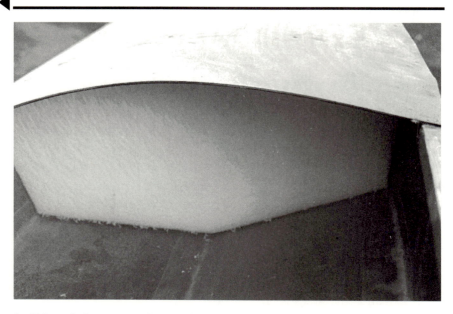

A foam bulkhead in place.

bulkheads because it's much easier to install, and it provides additional buoyancy. Closed-cell foam is manufactured in various grades and densities. Choose a type that's flexible but firm and has fairly small cells. Foam resembling the type used in running-shoe insoles is ideal. Many kayak shops carry closed-cell foam because it's used extensively to pad whitewater kayak cockpits. Don't use open-cell foam that absorbs water or stiff insulation-type foam that will crack and crumble. The price of closed-cell foam varies wildly, so shop around; industrial-plastics suppliers seem to have the best prices.

Plywood bulkheads are more trouble to make. I've installed the bulkhead and deck beam in this kayak prior to taping the hull.

One-quarter-inch plywood can also be used for bulkheads. But ply-wood bulkheads are more trouble to fit; you can't squeeze them into place as you can foam.

If you're installing the bulkheads while building your boat, fit them after the deck beams and carlins are in place. If retrofitting an existing boat, cutting the hatch openings first makes it easier to fit the bulkheads.

The shape of the bulkheads will depend on their position. Some paddlers prefer the after bulkhead be directly behind the seat; others like enough room behind the seat to carry spare clothes, a lunch, and other supplies. The position of the forward bulkhead is deter-mined largely by the length of your legs.

Start by making cardboard templates that fit in the position of the bulkheads. If you're installing foam bulkheads, the template need not be particularly accurate, since you'll cut the foam ¼ inch or so over-size and squeeze it into place for a perfect fit. Templates for plywood bulkheads, on the other hand, must be as accurate as possible. When you're satisfied with the fit and position of the templates, trace their shapes onto the foam or plywood. Cut closed-cell foam to shape with a large serrated knife or with your sabersaw fitted with a very long blade; cut plywood bulkheads as you would a hull panel. Foam bulk-heads are pushed into place and glued with 3M 5200 marine caulk. Plywood bulkheads should be glassed as if taping a hull seam.

If you're installing bulkheads in a boat that will be used only for short day-trips, hatches may be unnecessary. However, some means of ventilating the ends of the kayak is necessary to allow moisture to evaporate. The simplest solution is to drill a large hole in each bulk-head that can be plugged with a cork or dowel when the boat is used; this plug should be removed when the boat is stored. Another approach is to install a marine-type inspection plate (available at marine stores) on each bulkhead; these have the added advantage of allowing small items to be stored in the bow and stern compartments. Of course, the plates should be removed whenever the boat is stored.

Hatches

Hatches are necessary to allow access to the areas behind the bulk-heads. However, many hatches are not completely waterproof; the ones I've designed for my boats aren't waterproof. But before you return this volume to your bookseller in disgust, let me assure you that the vast majority of the hatches on plastic and fiberglass kayaks are not completely waterproof either. This isn't as tragic as it sounds because prudent paddlers will keep their gear in waterproof cases and dry-bags. In a day of paddling, the few ounces of water that find their way past most hatches will not noticeably affect the kayak's buoyancy, but your new Nikon will definitely be ruined. It's always safer to assume that any hatch leaks.

If you insist on truly watertight hatches, you can install those ugly plastic marine inspection plates; they even come in rectangular and clear models now. Or you can use the excellent, though equally ugly, British VCP rubber hatches. These are available as kits consisting of the hatch cover and a rim; they are for fiberglass kayaks, but they can be easily adapted to a wooden deck.

This hatch cover may not be 100 percent watertight, but it does a surprisingly good job. The seal is just closed-cell foam weather stripping, like you'd use on your windows.

Two nylon straps with Fastex buckles hold the hatch in place.

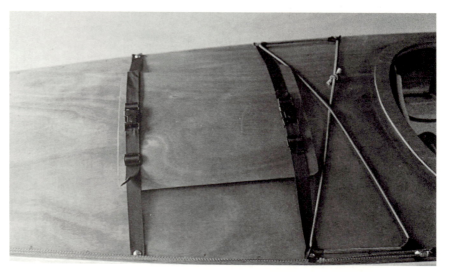

The hatch covers used for all three of our boats are identical. They are squares of plywood that are glued to frames with the same camber as the deck's. Wide weather stripping that's glued to the hatch cover's perimeter seals the hatch cover to the deck. Nylon straps screwed to the deck and sheer clamps hold the hatch covers in place.

The plans in Chapter 5 contain templates for the bow- and after-hatch cutouts. (You'll have to redraw them at full scale if you are using only the plans reproduced in this book.) Draw a light centerline on the deck in the area of the hatches. Line up the centerlines on the templates with the centerline on the boat and trace the cutouts. Drill a starter hole for your sabersaw blade, then cut out the openings. Remember, foam bulkheads are 3 inches thick; don't cut into them.

Make two frames for each hatch cover from short pieces of lattice, tracing the curve of the deck onto the lattice strips and cutting them to shape with a sabersaw. The frames should just fit into the deck opening. Glue the hatch frames onto the bottom of the hatch covers with thickened epoxy resin. The frames fit athwartship about 1½ inches from the edge of the hatch cover; use several clamps to hold the hatch cover to the frames. Fore-and-aft frames, sort of minicarlins, can be added to further stiffen the hatch cover.

Glue the foam weather stripping (bought at hardware or autoparts stores) underneath the perimeter of the hatch cover, as shown in the photo on page 114. Use the thickest and widest weather stripping you can find; ¼- x ⅜-inch closed-cell, self-adhesive weather stripping is my current favorite.

After the deck has been varnished, attach the hatch straps to the sheer clamps with ¾-inch screws and finish washers. The straps should be about two feet long so that they can be extended to hold down bulky gear stowed on deck. Fold about 1 inch of each strap over itself and melt the screw hole in it with a nail heated over a flame. Screw the straps into the sheer clamp so that the straps lay on the hatch covers. Finally, attach the buckles to the straps.

Another attractive hatch design seen on wooden kayaks consists of a hatch cover the same size as the hatch cut-out. This type of hatch rests on, and seals to, a frame glued to the underside of the deck. It can be designed to fit perfectly flush with the deck, giving the kayak a very sleek appearance. Hatches of this type are usually held closed by small swiveling latches, as seen in the photos.

If you're designing your own kayak, give the placement of the hatches some thought: when the hatches are located near the bulkheads, the deck in this area will remain quite stiff, but it will be diffi-

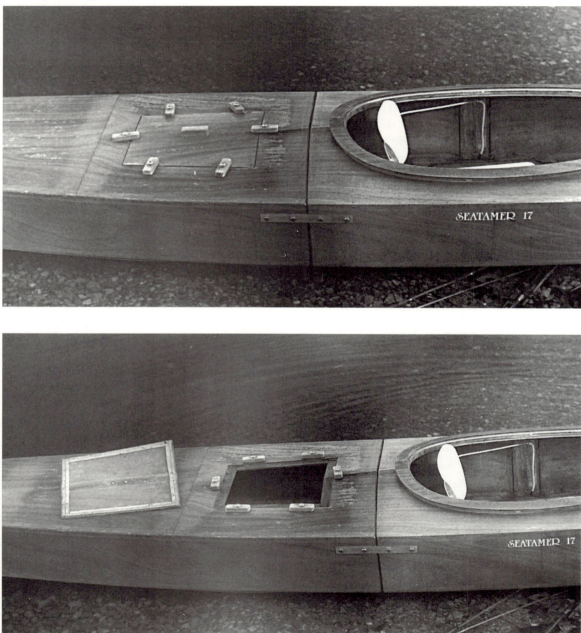

This flush-type hatch is on a South Shore Boatworks' 17-foot Sea Tamer kayak. Note the fiberglass seat unit.

cult to reach gear that's slid to the ends of the boat. On the other hand, if the hatches are located farther toward the kayak's ends, the deck loses some rigidity, but it's easier to reach the gear in the bow and stern.

Rudders

Rudders and rudder kits are available from many kayak shops and mail-order catalogs. They are usually designed to be retrofitted to a specific model of plastic or fiberglass kayak, but with a little fiddling, they can usually be adapted to a wooden kayak. I favor Feathercraft and Aquaterra rudders, which are very similar to each other in appearance and operation.

Rudder Mounts

Just locating a rudder mount that fits your kayak might be the biggest obstacle to installing a rudder. If possible, find the mount before installing the deck. If it is to be screwed to the hull, then backing plates should be glued into position before putting down the deck.

Manufacturers of plastic and fiberglass kayaks have specially designed metal mounts fabricated to fit their hulls. Scour the local kayak shops for a mount that's designed for another boat but that might fit yours. Welded mounts that are a close fit can often be bent

Much of the work in installing a rudder is figuring out how to mount it. The rudder mount farthest from the camera was made for a plastic kayak but fits this Yare when faired in with a little epoxy. The kayak closest to the camera has its rudder mounted in a hole that is drilled through the kayak's reinforced stern.

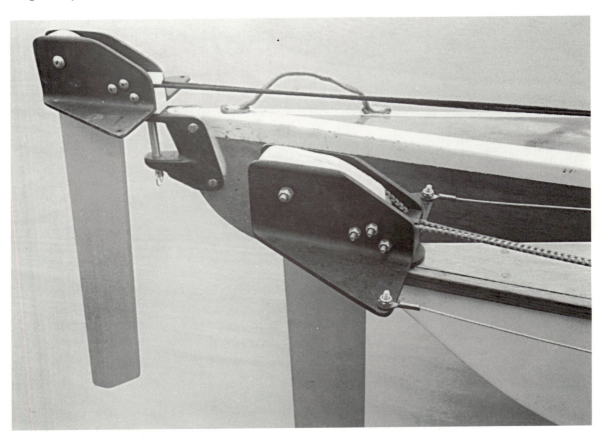

to fit. Cast mounts can sometimes be padded for a perfect fit. West Systems, the epoxy manufacturer, sells a high-strength filler (#404) that I've used to "sculpt in" rudder mounts for a custom fit. The cast-aluminum rudder mount in the photo is intended for an Aquaterra Chinook, but with a little epoxy magic it fits my wife's Yare—not perfectly, but it works.

A machinist or welder you know might be convinced to make a mount to your specifications. You could hire a machine shop to make one for you, but that might be expensive. Another option is to use stainless steel gudgeons that marine stores sell for mounting rudders on small sailing dinghies. With a little bending, these can be adapted to fit many kayaks.

A third option, and my favorite, is to forget about a separate mount and drill a hole in the deck and sheer clamps to accept the rudder pintle (or pin). To do this, cut off the last inch or so of the kayak. Drill a hole the same size as the pintle through the sheer clamps. It must be far enough forward of the newly truncated stern to let the rudder swing freely. Now this is the fun part: to prevent water from entering through this hole and to strengthen the mount, fill the end of the kayak with epoxy. Stand the kayak on end by leaning it against a tree or building; seal the hole you drilled with clear tape and pour in epoxy through the aft hatch or cockpit. Pour in the epoxy an ounce or two at a time; a large mass of curing resin can produce enough heat to melt the tape off the end of the hull! Continue adding epoxy until it's above the level of the mounting hole; you can see the level through the clear tape. When the epoxy has cured, redrill the hole and mount your rudder.

This type of mount will wear and have a sloppy fit after a few seasons. This can be remedied by brushing a little resin inside the hole with a cotton swab and then redrilling the hole. For an improved version, drill the hole a little oversized and glue in a bushing. The bushing can be a short length of metal tubing with the same inside diameter as the pintle's diameter, or your local machine shop can probably make a bronze bushing for a few dollars.

Cables and Deck Hardware

Mounting the rudder is only half the job; now you must run the steering cables, fit the rudder lifting line, and install sliding footbraces.

The steering cable housings will penetrate the deck about 2 feet forward of the rudder. The cables should bend as little as possible, therefore the points where the cables are attached to the rudder,

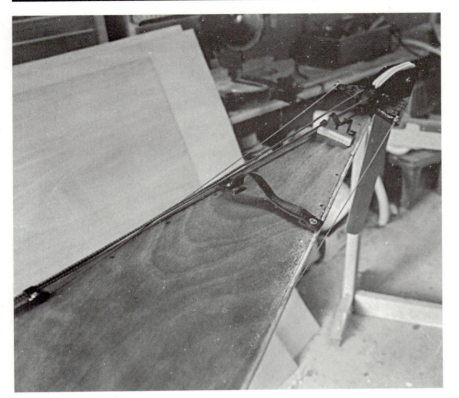

The rudder control cables enter the hull about two feet forward of the rudder. The V-shaped block holds the rudder in the center position when its raised onto the deck.

where they penetrate the deck, and where they pass through the bulkhead should be a straight line—more or less. Drill holes through the deck at an angle; then the cables won't bend sharply where they exit the holes. Seal the cable housing to the deck and to the bulkhead with 3M 5200 sealant or with clear-silicon caulk. Use plastic cable anchors to attach the housing to the deck, just aft of the exit holes; this will prevent the cable from shifting and breaking the caulked seal. Also attach the cable housing in several places inside the kayak.

Mount your footbraces as described in the previous chapter, and attach the cables to them. But first check that both footbraces are in the same position when the rudder is centered. The cables are usually attached to the footbraces with a swage. If you own or can borrow a swaging tool, use it to squeeze the swage shut; otherwise, use a pair of Vise-Grips or a large pair of pliers to squeeze the swage shut in several spots. Squeeze tightly so the cables won't come loose at a critical moment.

Most rudders are designed to lift out of the water by using a loop of

Sliding peddles, like these Keepers made by Aquaterra, control the rudder. Notice that the bulkhead is just forward of the slides; it hasn't been sealed to the hull yet.

line led to within the paddler's reach; pulling on one side of the loop raises the rudder, pulling on the other lowers it. The loop goes through an eye that is held in tension by a piece of elastic cord, as shown in the photo on page 121. The elastic cord prevents the loop from loosening and tightening as the rudder moves; it is fastened to a fitting beside the cockpit. The lifting and lowering loop should pass through the elastic cord's eye just behind the paddler as well as through two or three eyes, or cable anchors, along the kayak's gunwale. These can be attached with the same type of screws that hold the hatch-cover straps and grab handles.

It's handy to have a jam cleat on deck to secure the rudder's lifting loop in the up or down position. If you can't find a jam cleat in your kayak shop, they are available in most marine stores and catalogs. Screw the jam cleat to the sheer clamp, just behind the elastic cord's eye. You may also want to install a V-fitting to hold the rudder blade centered when it's in the on-deck position.

Skegs

Skegs are small fins added under the rear of a kayak's hull to improve its tracking. Skegs may be fixed, or they may retract like the centerboard on a sailboat. They can be made from aluminum plate or from thick plywood, glued and taped to the hull. If plywood is used for the skeg, it should be reinforced with fiberglass along its bottom. If

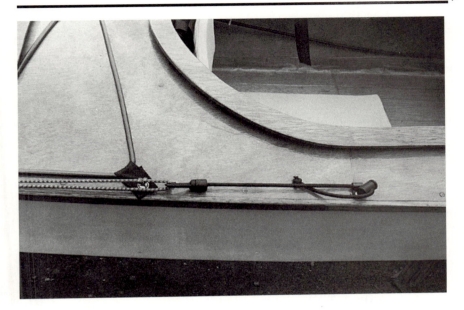

The thin, patterned line raises and lowers the rudder. The elastic cord and cord clamp tension the line and keep it within the paddler's reach.

you design a boat that seems deficient in holding a course, you may be able to "save" it by adding a small, fixed skeg.

Retractable skegs are favored over rudders by some paddlers; they seem particularly popular on English boats. Retractable skegs are used to improve the balance of a kayak without the complication of a rudder. I've never installed a retractable skeg, but kits for retrofitting them are available from some kayak stores.

Chapter 11
Finishing

'd succeeded in laying on five flawless coats of varnish. The kayak I was working on was to be displayed at a large outdoor equipment store to promote my seminar on kayak building. After painstakingly brushing on the sixth and final coat, I tiptoed out of the shop and locked the door. The next morning, I was ready to deliver my flawless new boat to the store, when I opened the shop to find that a squirrel had gotten inside and walked over my wet varnish.

The moral of this story is that the deck is stacked against you when trying to achieve a fine finish. You'll struggle against bubbles, runs, dust, kamikaze insects, and squirrels. But it's worth the trouble; nothing shows the beauty of a wooden boat like six coats of varnish. Unfortunately, it's tempting to rush through this stage of construction, telling yourself that you only want a functional boat. Before you

You can hardly see the squirrel tracks on the after deck. Achieving a yacht-quality finish takes lots of time and attention to detail, plus a little luck.

do, consider how much effort you've already put into the project.

You must apply some type of finish to your boat. A couple of coats of epoxy may look like varnish, but epoxy deteriorates in sunlight, turning milky and dull. The kayak needs to be protected with either paint or varnish. Most paddlers want to finish their hull, deck, and interior bright. (You'll also need to varnish inside your kayak; sunlight strikes there, too.)

However, there's an argument to be made for painting the hull. Paint holds up better than varnish, is more abrasion resistant, is easier to touch up, and does not require as many coats. In addition, you can use fairing compound to achieve a smoother, more efficient, and faster hull. Even large scratches or chips in the wood can be repaired with fairing compound and hidden under paint. But, surprisingly, surface irregularities and poor sanding seem more visible on a painted surface than a varnished one. I think this is because people are a little awestruck by shiny expanses of varnished wood, and they don't notice the surface details under the varnish. One last point: you can always paint over the varnish later, but there isn't much hope of varnishing over the paint.

Epoxy saturation fills the wood's grain that's been opened by bending. A foam roller applies a smooth, even coat.

Epoxy Saturation

Prior to varnishing or painting your kayak, saturate its hull with unthickened epoxy. The epoxy soaks into the wood, filling and reinforcing the wood's grain, particularly the grain opened by bending. Saturation adds a tough outer skin that increases the hull's abrasion resistance and strength. In addition, epoxy provides a smooth, clear base that adds depth to the final finish.

If I'm building a kayak that's to be infrequently used, I only epoxy saturate the hull, but if it's to be used in the ocean or for long trips, I'll apply epoxy to the deck as well. If you decide not to epoxy the deck, give it its initial coat of varnish now.

As mentioned earlier, epoxy doesn't flow or level well, so applying a smooth coat is difficult. Again, the best tool for applying epoxy is a foam roller. Roll a thin layer of epoxy over the entire surface; most of this first coat will be absorbed into the wood. Rollers tend to leave small bubbles on the epoxy's surface. These must be tipped-off by running a disposable foam or bristle brush over the fresh epoxy; just skim the surface with the brush's tip to pop the bubbles. Brush out any runs or drips, or you will have to sand them out later. When the epoxy has started to cure, roll on the second coat and, again, brush out any bubbles and runs. Be particularly careful to seal exposed plywood edges, such as the underside of the coaming; if water enters the plywood's core, it can cause problems later.

Any bubbles can be popped by tipping off the epoxy with a disposable brush. Run the brush very lightly over the entire surface.

Sheathing the Hull with Fiberglass

Many kayak builders routinely apply a layer of fiberglass to the kayak's hull for increased abrasion resistance, stiffness, and strength. If the kayak will be dragged across the beach or paddled in an area

with a rocky shoreline, sheathing with fiberglass is a good idea; if you're really tough on your boat, Kevlar cloth can be substituted for fiberglass.

But if you make a habit of getting out of your boat in ankle-deep water and not dragging it up the beach, you don't need a fiberglass-covered bottom. Not glassing the hull will save you a day's work and 4 to 6 pounds of weight. You've already applied two strips of heavy fiberglass tape to the exterior hull seams, so the most vulnerable areas are already protected. I don't glass my kayaks, and they seem to hold up very well; of course, I'm more careful with them than I might be if the hulls were glassed.

If you decide to fiberglass your hull, you'll need a length of 4- or 6-ounce fiberglass cloth as long as the boat. Start by turning the hull upside down and wiping it with acetone to remove any dust or chemical contamination. Stretch the fiberglass cloth over the hull and run your hands along it to smooth out the wrinkles. At the bow and stern, cut long darts in the cloth, so its shape approximates that of the hull panels.

Use staples, push pins, or masking tape to secure the cloth to the gunnel and keel line. Let the excess cloth just hang below the boat. Rather than brushing on the epoxy, pour it along the keel line and work it into the cloth with a squeegee. Completely saturate the cloth as you did the tape. Work fast—you have a large area to cover. When the epoxy coat has started to cure, trim off the excess cloth hanging below the hull. Apply two or more additional resin coats to fill the cloth's weave.

Sanding and Fairing

No matter how carefully you rolled, brushed, or squeegeed the epoxy resin onto your hull and deck, it will not be perfectly smooth. And even if the surface was perfect, varnish or paint won't adhere properly to unsanded epoxy. You'll need to spend at least a few hours sanding and fairing.

Before you start sanding, wash the boat with detergent and water to remove the surface film that curing epoxy leaves; detergent that contains ammonia works best. This waxy film, called *amine blush*, clogs sandpaper and prevents paint and varnish from drying. Two thorough washes with a sponge and warm, soapy water followed by a rinse should remove it.

Use 80-grit paper on your sander, or 120-grit if sanding by hand. Most of the sanding will be concentrated at the seams; the major part

Sanding is best done outside. Wear a mask: who knows what epoxy dust will do to your brain?

of the hull should be almost smooth, except for runs in the epoxy. Sand the entire hull, giving the most attention to the seams and the edges of the tape. When you've finished, there should be no shiny spots remaining to indicate a low or unsanded area. If you accidently sand through the epoxy layer—and you probably will—recoat the area and sand it later.

Some builders like to roll on several more coats of epoxy after the initial sanding. This builds up a deep glasslike base for the varnish. Of course, they have to sand the subsequent coats. I've done this on one kayak, and the finish is very impressive—but it sure was a lot of work.

After sanding, you'll need to wash the kayak again to remove the sanding dust. Epoxy dust is tenacious stuff that won't just rinse off with a casual spray. You need to go over the boat several times with a wet towel or sponge.

If the hull is to be painted, use fairing compound to fill any low spots or surface pinholes. The compound is a fast-setting, easily sanded, two-part epoxy or polyester putty. It's available at any marine store. Because it's not clear, fairing compound can't be used under varnish. But you can brush on extra epoxy resin to fill low spots under varnish.

Apply the fairing compound with a putty knife or the applicators available from auto-parts stores that are used for bodywork. (They work as well as the much more expensive brands sold at marine stores.) Mix the fairing compound on translucent-plastic pallets sold for this purpose, or on pieces of stiff cardboard. But prior to mixing the fairing compound, circle all the spots that need filling with a pencil. When this is done, apply the mixture to any area that seems low; spread it with the applicator as if spackling a wall, and pay particular attention to the edges of taped seams. Some fairing compounds set up within a few minutes, therefore be prepared to work fast.

Sand the compound with your finishing sander, then with 120-grit paper on a rubber sanding block. Normally, I'll circle a kayak half a dozen times, repeatedly marking low spots, spreading fairing compound, and sanding it. If you learn not to apply more compound than is necessary to fill a depression, it only takes about 15 minutes, to spread and sand the stuff; this doesn't include curing time. If you're after a truly professional paint job, wet sand the entire hull with 220-grit paper after fairing.

Choosing a Varnish

Use only high-quality marine varnish on your kayak. Marine varnishes have ultraviolet filters that allow them to resist the deteriorating effects of sunlight longer than other varnishes. Stick to established marine brands such as Z-Spar, Epifanes, Interlux, and Woolsey. Varnishing isn't easy; don't make it tougher by using an inferior household varnish.

Each of the above-mentioned manufacturers makes several types of varnish. There are subtle differences between all the types as well as the brands. Much of varnishing involves getting a feel for the varnish you're using, so don't change brands or types once you've got the hang of it. I use Z-Spar's Captain's Varnish for 90 percent of my work. If I'm feeling bold, I might use Z-Spar's Flagship varnish on the final coats, since it builds a little thicker. However, I'd never use it as a first coat because it doesn't dry well over epoxy. See what I mean about learning to use one type?

Two-part polyurethane varnishes have recently become popular. They dry very hard, are abrasion resistant, resist sunlight well, and are compatible with epoxy. Despite these advantages, many builders still prefer traditional oil-based varnishes. I've tried two-part polyurethanes, but I'm still undecided about them because they're very expensive, harder to apply than oil-based varnish, and relatively untested. This type of varnish is essentially a clear paint, so if you use it, follow the instructions for applying two-part polyurethane paint.

Choosing Paint

Two-part polyurethane should probably be called three-part polyurethane because it must be thinned with a special solvent. It's best applied with a foam roller and tipped out with a foam brush.

Of the types of paint I've tried, the three I'll cover here are the most satisfactory. One of these should suit most builders; they include latex house paint, marine enamel, and two-part polyurethane.

Though you may snicker, latex house paint is actually not a bad choice; it is cheap, readily available in almost any color, and easy to apply. Of course, it's not too glossy or abrasion resistant, but if applied carefully and allowed to dry for a week or so before the boat is used, you'd be surprised. I've had boatshop pundits ask if it was marine enamel or polyurethane I'd used on my latex-coated boat. Despite the instructions on the can, latex paint seems to take weeks to truly dry; you can use your boat after 48 hours, but try not to scrape the still-soft paint. If you want a quick-and-dirty paint job, try latex; at least you can clean your tools and brushes in water.

Marine enamels are the traditional oil-based paints. They give a hard, reasonably glossy, abrasion-resistant finish. They are not expensive, as marine paints go, and are available in many colors. On the down side, some marine enamels don't dry well over epoxy. Many builders prefer the one-part polyurethanes to traditional enamels because they are harder and glossier.

I've started using two-part, or linear, polyurethane. It's much harder and glossier than any other paint I've used. In fact, I'm told that manufacturers have painted their fiberglass show boats with it because it's glossier than gelcoat. Unfortunately, two-part polyurethane is more expensive and harder to apply than most other paints. The extreme gloss and relative thinness of this paint brings out every flaw in the underlying surface, so you must prepare your hull with fanatical care before applying it.

There are numerous other paints on the market, and new ones are being introduced constantly. Most marine paint companies have technical representatives that will happily discuss the merits and application of their products with you. But not all paints are compatible with epoxy resin, so if you're using a new paint, first coat a small area as a test.

In choosing the color of your paint, consider whether you'll be able to get more of it when you need to touch up a scrape. White paint is always available; "minty teal" will (hopefully) be discontinued soon. Actually, there are several reasons to choose a white hull: kayaks painted a light color are cooler in the sun; many paddlers think that light-colored hulls look better with a varnished deck; scratches don't show up as easily on a white hull; and white is visible from a distance.

Tools for Finishing

The top professional yacht painters and varnishers I've met apply finishes either with a cheap, disposable foam brush and roller or with a top-quality, very expensive, badger bristle brush; they don't use anything in between. So I've switched to using disposable foam brushes and rollers; not only are they cheaper, but you don't have to clean them. I still keep a badger bristle brush around for little touch-up jobs. If you object to using disposable brushes for environmental reasons, think about how much brush cleaner you'd use to clean a bristle brush in the course of painting your kayak. The large, relatively flat surfaces of a kayak are difficult to coat with a brush; therefore, consider using a foam roller. It's a little tricky using a roller with varnish, but once you get the hang of it, it's very fast and effective.

Paint and varnish can also be applied with a spray gun, but it requires special skills that most of us don't have. If you decide to spray, contact the manufacturer for specific instructions. Some marine paints are incredibly toxic and a positive-pressure respirator must be worn while spraying.

You may have noticed a paint stripe covering the hull-to-deck joint on some kayaks; these are very difficult to paint without using masking tape. Use the plastic 3M "fine-line" tape, not regular paper masking tape. The trick to getting a nice clean line is to press the edge

Use masking tape to prevent varnish from seeping onto your paint.

down firmly, so paint can't seep under it. Don't leave masking tape in place for more than a couple of days, or it may take two more days to remove it.

Applying Varnish and Paint

The first thing you should do prior to painting or varnishing is to read the directions on the can. No one knows more about that type of paint or varnish than its manufacturer, and the advice is right there in front of you. Most manufacturers also give out free literature full of tips on applying their products; Interlux even includes a how-to audiotape with one of their paints. Most of the instructions are devoted primarily to preparing the surface prior to painting—I know you've probably heard this before, but it's important enough to repeat: preparation really is 90 percent of a good finish job.

Varnish and paint are very sensitive to temperature and humidity. If possible, varnish or paint only on warm dry days. If you're working outdoors, put the finish on early so it's almost dry before the dew starts to form in the evening. Avoid painting or varnishing outdoors on very hot days, cold days, windy days, or when there are lots of bugs around. Lastly, if there's any chance it might rain, don't varnish outdoors; if it's already raining don't even varnish indoors.

Whether you're painting or varnishing, sand lightly between coats. If applying a two-part polyurethane, wet-sand before the final coat.

It may sound as if there are only a couple of days a year when you can paint or varnish, but here are a couple of tricks you can use to expand the finishing "window." On cool days, below 60 degrees, add a little Japan drier to your varnish or oil-based paint to make it dry faster. On hot days, above 80 degrees, thin your varnish or paint with a little turpentine or marine penetrol to make it brush easier. These tricks don't work with polyurethanes, so follow the manufacturer's directions.

There's nothing like a few coats of varnish to bring out the beauty of your wooden deck.

Prior to painting or varnishing, wash your boat again to remove the amine blush that has formed while you were sanding as well as remaining traces of sanding dust. Consider wetting the floor of your shop so you won't kick up any dust while working. Finally, wipe down the boat with a tack cloth. Two-part polyurethane is very sensitive to impurities, so if you'll be using it also wipe down the hull with solvent-wash.

Never use varnish or paint directly out of the can; instead, pour as much as you'll need for one coat into a clean cup or can. And when you finish, don't think of pouring the remainder back into the can. If you'll be using a foam roller, pour the paint or varnish into a clean roller tray.

Don't overload a roller with paint or varnish. Try to apply thin even coats over the entire surface. Work quickly so you're always rolling into a wet edge rather than into paint or varnish that has started to set. Have an assistant tip off the finish by lightly running a foam brush over it to pop the bubbles and smooth out the coat. If you're working alone, you'll need to hurry to tip off the finish yourself. It's common to get a surface finish that looks stippled, or like an orange peel, when using a roller. I believe this is caused by trying to apply too thin a coat or by a dusty surface.

If you are using a brush, put on a thin coat with long, quick brush strokes, working each stroke into the coating you just put down. Keep looking back for spots you missed or runs starting to form. These can be repaired if caught soon, but don't go over paint or varnish that's already started to skim over. Apply the finish across the grain and then tip off with the direction of the grain. Don't lay on too thick a coat or it won't fully dry; two thin coats are always better than one thick coat.

When you're finished, check for squirrels and lock your shop.

I usually wait two days after applying the first coat of varnish, then overnight between subsequent coats. Sand lightly between coats; wipe off the sanding dust with wet paper towels and then with a tack cloth. You'll need at least four coats of varnish for a good finish, six or seven for a yacht-quality finish. After ten coats even your most jaded plastic-boat paddling friends will want wooden kayaks.

Chapter 12
Fitting Out

Your kayak is almost finished, but before you paddle off into the sunset, take a few hours to add those details that make paddling safer, more convenient, and more comfortable. These include deck grab loops, deck tie-downs, a bilge pump, compass, and cockpit padding. Because you will also need a paddle, I'll describe two that are easy to make and pleasant to use.

Bow and Stern Handles

Grab handles at the bow and stern are an important safety feature that should be installed on every kayak. They allow you to easily hang on to a kayak when rescuing someone or when wet-exiting. Handles can also be used to tow the kayak, to tie the boat on a car rack, as attachment points for a painter, and they are a convenient means for two people to carry the boat. The grab loops must be strong and securely attached to the kayak: just consider how much force is put on them when you manhandle a fully loaded or flooded kayak.

The simplest way to install grab handles is to drill holes a few inches from the tips of the bow and stern and then pass loops of line through them. It's best to drill these holes partially through the sheer clamp and then fiberglass a piece of plastic or metal tubing into the hole. The tube will reinforce the hole and prevent water from entering the kayak. Another way to waterproof the hole is to epoxy the line to the hull, but the epoxy will eventually crack and leak and the line will be difficult to replace. If you plan to install your grab handles in either of these ways, it's easier to do so before finishing the boat.

Grab handles can be simple loops of line epoxied into a hole drilled in the bow and stern.

Good grab handles can be made from tubular nylon webbing or strap by screwing 8-inch lengths to the deck and sheer clamp. Tubular tape is softer and easier on your hands than the flat straps you may have used to hold down your hatches. The tape is available at outdoor and climbing shops in various widths and colors. Attach the grab handles with 1-inch #10 screws and finish washers.

When building the Pocomoke and other kayaks that have a traditional appearance, I screw bronze flange-eyes to the deck at the bow and stern. The grab loops and painter can simply be tied through these. The flange eyes should be of the heavy-duty type that take four screws rather than two. All four screws must bite into the sheer clamps or they will eventually pull out.

Grab handles made from tubular nylon webbing are easy to install and easy on your hands.

Bronze pad eyes add a nice touch to a traditionally styled kayak like this Pocomoke.

Deck Tie-Downs

Deck tie-downs hold gear and, more importantly, a paddle and paddle float when performing a wet reentry.

Many paddlers find it convenient to carry gear, such as water bottles, charts (in a waterproof bag), a spare paddle, and a paddle float, on deck. The deck tie-downs also hold your paddle and paddle float in position during a wet reentry. The most common tie-down system consists of several elastic cords that are crisscrossed over the deck.

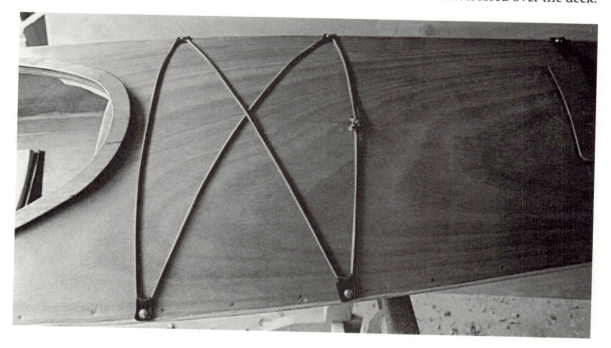

Run the elastic cord through plastic or metal eyelets (available at marine stores) or through loops of nylon strap that are screwed to the sheer clamps. If you use nylon loops, add a finish washer over the nylon to prevent the loop from pulling off the screw head. I normally use ¼-inch elastic cord for deck tie-downs; it's a little thicker than you'll see on some kayaks, but the cord holds the gear more securely and only costs a few cents more.

Compasses, Bilge Pumps, and Other Deck-mounted Gear

One of the great things about having a wooden boat is that it's easy to modify. Compasses, bilge pumps, fishing-rod holders, water-bottle holders, or most anything else you think of can be mounted on deck. In most cases, all you need to do is glue a backing plate under the deck and screw your new toy to it.

If you decide to install a compass, consider mounting it on the forward-hatch cover. This position has a couple of advantages: the compass is far enough forward that you see it over gear stowed under the tie-downs, and is easier on your eyes than trying to read a compass that's too close to the cockpit. To make sure that nothing happens to the compass, the forward hatch can be replaced with a plain hatch when you transport the boat or leave it unattended on your roof rack.

This compass is mounted on the forward hatch. The hatch and compass can be replaced with a plain hatch when the kayak is left on a car rack.

Bilge pumps are another vital safety feature on sea kayaks. You can carry a hand-held pump in the cockpit, under the deck tie-downs or you can install a diaphragm-type pump on deck. If you decide for a deck-mounted pump, position it near the aft-deck beam and glue a generously sized backing plate under the deck. The plate is needed because you can exert substantial pressure on the deck when operating a diaphragm-type pump.

Cockpit Padding

A comfortable cockpit is essential to a pleasant paddling experience. I am convinced that almost any cockpit can be made comfortable with the addition of closed-cell foam padding. Closed-cell foam also provides extra flotation, and, since it doesn't absorb water, it can be wiped dry before you get in your boat.

Half-inch foam is available from kayak shops, outdoor stores, and camping stores (where it's sold as pads for sleeping bags). Glue the foam into place with contact cement. The cement is quick and easy to use and not very strong. If you don't use too much of it, you can rip

Closed-cell foam of the type used for sleeping bag pads is perfect for padding cockpits.

the foam out and replace it when it starts to get flat. Pad your backrest, seat, and the area under the deck where you brace your knees. But remember that raising the height of your seat adversely affects the kayak's stability.

These paddles are easy to make, light, and pleasant to use.

Paddles

When choosing a type and length of paddle, it's wise to try out as many different types as possible. Generally, narrow-bladed paddles and paddles with small blade areas are less tiring to use on long trips and in windy conditions. An advantage to paddles with larger blade areas and modern asymmetrical designs is that they allow more control and higher speeds. Shorter paddles and smaller blade areas result in a higher stroke rate than larger-blade-area paddles. Feathered paddles, that is paddles with the blades set at right angles to each other, are more efficient in head winds, but they can cause wrist problems.

The length of your paddle will be influenced by your build and paddling style, but here are some starting points. For narrower boats, such as the Yare, a 7-foot 6-inch-long paddle is about right; for wider kayaks, like the Pocomoke, a paddle about 8 feet long is best.

Kayak paddles are expensive, and well-made wooden paddles can be difficult to find. Fortunately, you can build a serviceable kayak paddle in about six hours. These paddles are made by gluing plywood blades onto solid-wood shafts. With a little whittling and planing, they can be made very light, attractive, and efficient. I admit that I usually use a "store-bought" paddle, but I've made several spare paddles for friends who want to borrow one of my kayaks. I've also made two very long paddles for my Klepper double kayak.

The blades for these paddles are made from ¼-inch or 4mm marine plywood. Rather than use regular ¼-inch plywood I prefer to laminate two layers of 3mm plywood—some is always left over from kayak hulls or decks. This method produces a stiffer blade with more laminations. The paddles' shafts are made from 1¼-inch fir closet poles. You might need to look through a whole pile of poles to find one suitable for a paddle shaft. Look for a pole that's light; straight; has tight, straight grain; and has no knots. You can also carve the shaft from a solid spruce 2 x 2. Another type of shaft can be made by laminating two pieces of 1-inch half-round molding to a 1- x ¼-inch spacer. The ¼-inch-thick blade slides between the moldings and up to the spacer.

I've also seen homemade paddles carved from solid boards, but I don't care for them; they aren't easy to make, and they are often too narrow and heavy. The best wooden paddles are carved from laminated solid-wood strips; they are my favorite type of paddle, so I'll happily pay an expert to make them for me.

The only special tool you might need to make paddles is a spokeshave. A spokeshave allows you to quickly and easily shape the scooped-out area onto which the blade is glued. If you're buying a spokeshave, spend a bit more for the type with knobs that adjust the blade's depth. You can also carve out the scoop with a rasp, draw knife, belt sander, or, if you're a skilled carver, your pocket knife.

Plans for Two Paddles

These plans were originally drawn as full-size patterns, so the builder could simply trace the shape onto the blade blank. Because they couldn't be reproduced here at full size, I've added some dimensions that you can use to make full-size drawings. Or you could take this book to a large-copy shop and have the plans reproduced at full size. (Don't try this with kayak plans; there will be far too much distortion.)

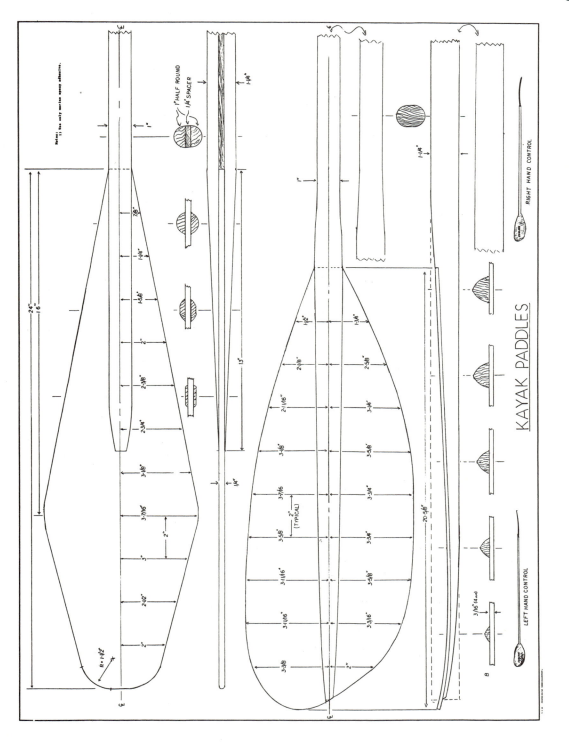

KAYAK PADDLES

RIGHT HAND CONTROL

LEFT HAND CONTROL

Note: Use only marine epoxy adhesive.

1" HALF ROUND

1/4" SPACER

The diamond-blade paddle can be made in a couple of hours from molding and lattice available at any lumberyard and a plywood blade. Be sure the weight of the clamps does not bend the shaft as the epoxy cures.

Making the Diamond-Blade Paddle

This paddle is well suited to general touring. It's based roughly on traditional paddles of the Far North. The blade area is moderate, so it's not tiring to use on longer trips.

The paddle shaft is composed of two pieces of pine or spruce 1-inch half-round molding and a 1- x ¼-inch piece of lattice, which are available at most lumberyards. The lattice may be replaced with a mahogany or other dark-wood strip to provide an attractive, contrasting stripe. The paddle blade is made of ¼-inch marine-grade plywood.

Cut the two half-round moldings 22 inches shorter than the overall paddle length. Cut the lattice or spacer strip 48 inches shorter than the overall paddle length. With your block plane, taper the ends of the half-round molding, as shown on the plan. Next, copy the blade's shape from the plan onto your plywood and cut the plywood to shape.

Coat the flat sides of the half-round molding with thickened marine-epoxy resin and assemble the paddle as shown on the plan. Clamp the parts together and wipe up any epoxy that's squeezed out of the joints. After the epoxy has cured, sand the paddle and apply a coat of unthickened epoxy to the entire paddle.

Making the Asymmetrical Paddle

Asymmetrical paddles are designed to relieve the twisting or torque common to many wider paddles. This is a light and efficient paddle designed for touring or racing. It may be built feathered or unfeathered. Because it involves more carving, this paddle is a bit more difficult to make than the diamond-blade model.

A spokeshave makes it easy to carve light and attractive paddle shafts from 1¼-inch spruce or fir dowels.

The shaft is a 1¼-inch dowel or closet pole, either fir or spruce. The blade can be 4mm or ¼-inch plywood. Start by cutting the dowel to the proper length. Use your sabersaw to rough shape the ends to the pattern shown on the plan. Use the sketches at the bottom of the plan to properly orient a feathered paddle's blades. With your spoke-shave, carefully carve the "scoop"; measure the shape frequently so you don't cut too far. Also, be careful to maintain the proper alignment between the shaft's two ends. Use a block plane to shape the back of the shaft, and then your spokeshave to narrow the throat and the hand grip. Work slowly and stop often to compare your work to the plan.

Lay out the blades to the shape shown on the plans and cut them out with your sabersaw. Glue the blades to the shaft with thickened marine-epoxy resin. Use several large clamps to hold the blade to the shaft. When the epoxy has cured, sand the paddle and coat it with a layer of unthickened epoxy.

Finishing Paddles

If you're hard on your paddles, it may be a good idea to apply a layer of thin (4-ounce) fiberglass cloth to the blades. This greatly increases a paddle's durability. Stretch the cloth over the blade and brush on several coats of epoxy resin to saturate it. When the epoxy has cured, sand the blade and apply another coat of epoxy to fill the cloth's pattern.

After the epoxy coating has cured, wash the paddle in soap and water to remove the amine blush. Sand the paddle again and finish it with several coats of marine varnish.

Go Paddling

Launch your new kayak in calm water. Some kayaks, such as the Yare, are high-performance boats that may seem quite tippy if you're not used to them. After a little practice, this shouldn't be a problem, but it's best to get used to these boats on calm water.

If this is your first kayak, please get a paddling and safety lesson. You should, at the very least, know how to reenter a kayak in deep water by using a paddle float and about the dangers of hypothermia. Be sure to always take your personal flotation device, a paddle float, and a bilge pump. If your boat isn't fitted with bulkheads, it must be fitted with flotation bags; these plastic buoyancy bags fit into the bow and stern and are available at any kayak shop. If you're paddling in cold water, wear a wetsuit or, even better, a dry suit. It only takes a few minutes for hypothermia to set in if you wet-exit.

Storing and Maintaining Your Kayak

Ensure your kayak's long life by storing it under cover. If you don't have room at home, you might consider building a covered outdoor rack, renting space at a local boat house, or keeping the boat in a neighbor's garage. I store several kayaks by suspending them from the rafters in my shop; more kayaks are stored on top of the rafters and are reached by a little door I installed just below the roof's peak. Do what you must, but don't leave your wooden boat outdoors for months at a time.

Always wipe the water out of your boat after each trip; leaving standing water in a wooden boat is asking for rot. Store your kayak with the hatches off and without wet gear lying in it. Like all wooden boats, your kayak will need a bit of maintenance to ensure its long life. Inevitably, it will get scratched and banged up a little. If a scratch

or ding penetrates into the wood, cover it with varnish as soon as the wood dries out. If the scratch is deep, level it out with epoxy first.

After a year or two of use, the varnish starts looking a little dull. This is the time to sand it lightly and brush on an additional coat. If you neglect it too long, it could crack and lift; then only a complete sanding down to the epoxy and new varnish will bring it back. Actually, taking a few hours each spring to lay on a fresh coat of varnish can be a strangely rewarding experience.

Clay Corry considers paddling off into the sunset.

Appendix A
Further Reading

Books About Kayak Building

▼ Dyson, George. *Baidarka*. Anchorage, AK: Alaska Northwest Books, 1986.
Building kayaks based on native designs from aluminum tubing and nylon.

▼ Gougeon Brothers. *The Gougeon Brothers on Boat Construction*. Bay City, MI: Gougeon Brothers, Inc., 1985.
The bible of wood-epoxy construction.

▼ Putz, George. *Wood and Canvas Kayak Building*. Camden, ME: International Marine, 1990.
Canvas-on-frame kayaks.

▼ Snaith, Skip. *Canoes and Kayaks for the Backyard Builder*. Camden, ME: International Marine, 1989.
Plywood boats built on forms.

▼ Wittman, Rebecca J. *Brightwork*. Camden, ME: International Marine, 1990.
Looking for the ultimate finish.

Periodicals

▼ *Atlantic Coastal Kayaker*
29 Burley Street, Wenham, MA 01984

▼ *Boatbuilder*
P.O. Box 3000, Denville, NJ 07834

▼ *Fine Woodworking*
The Taunton Press, P.O. Box 5506, Newtown, CT 06470

▼ *messing about in Boats*
29 Burley Street, Wenham, MA 01984

▼ *Sea Kayaker*
6327 Seaview Avenue NW, Seattle, WA 98107

▼ *WoodenBoat*
P.O. Box 78, Brooklin, ME 04616

Appendix B
List of Suppliers

This is a list of companies I've done business with and can recommend, or that have been recommended to me by friends or by other boatbuilders. Other suppliers can be found by looking through the ads in *WoodenBoat* magazine. Companies that sell paddles, spray skirts, and other gear often advertise in *Sea Kayaker* magazine.

▼ Boulter Plywood Corporation, 24 Broadway, Somerville, MA 02145 (plywood)

▼ Chesapeake Light Craft, 1805 George Ave., Annapolis, MD 21401 (plywood, epoxy, rudders, parts and accessories)

▼ Chesapeake Marine Fasteners, 10 Willow Street, Annapolis, MD 21401 (fasteners)

▼ Clark Craft, 16 Aqua Lane, Tonawanda, NY 14150 (epoxy, fiberglass, fasteners)

▼ Defender Industries, 255 Main Street, P.O. Box 820, New Rochelle, NY 10802 (epoxy, fiberglass cloth, and a wide range of supplies)

▼ Eden Saw, 211 Seton Road, Port Townsend, WA 98368 (lumber and plywood)

▼ Flounder Bay Boat Lumber, 1019 3rd Street, Anacortes, WA 98221 (plywood, solid wood, epoxies, and related supplies)

▼ Garrett Wade, 161 Avenue of the Americas, New York, NY 10013 (tools)

▼ Great River Outfitters, 3721 Shallow Brook, Bloomfield Hills, MI 48302 (accessories, including VCP hatch kits, rudders, skeg kits, and backstraps)

▼ Jamestown Distributors, 28 Narraganset Avenue, Jamestown, RI 02835, (epoxy, hardware, fiberglass tape, and a wide range of boatbuilding supplies and tools)

▼ Harbor Sales, 1401 Russell Street, Baltimore, MD 21230 (plywood)

▼ Hudson Marine Plywood, P.O. Box 1184, Elkhart, IN 46515 (plywood)

▼ M. L. Condon Company, 260 Ferris Avenue, White Plains, NY 10603 (lumber and plywood)

▼ Mas Epoxies, P.O. Box 518, Pennsauken, NJ 08110 (epoxy and related supplies)

▼ System Three, P.O. Box 70436, Seattle, WA 98107 (epoxy and related supplies)

▼ The Wooden Boat Shop, 1007 N.E. Boat Street, Seattle, WA 98105 (wood, tools, supplies, hardware)

Appendix C
Plans and Kits

▼ Chesapeake Light Craft, 1805 George Ave., Annapolis, MD 21401; 410-267-0137

▼ Clark Craft, 16 Aqua Lane, Tonawanda, NY 14150

▼ Dennis Davis Designs, 9 Great Burrow Rise, Northam, Bideford, Devon EX39 1TB, England

▼ Heritage Wooden Boats, P.O. Box 641, Bacliff, TX 77518

▼ Lake Watercraft, RR #3, Box 845, Wiscasset, ME 04578

▼ The WoodenBoat Store, P.O. Box 78, Brooklin, ME 04616

▼ The Wooden Boat Shop, 1007 N.E. Boat St., Seattle, WA 98105

Appendix D
More Designs
by the Author

A s I wrote earlier, the designs I describe in this book are not suited to all, perhaps not even to most, paddlers. But I suspect many of you will want to employ the building techniques I've illustrated without going to the considerable bother of designing your own kayak. So, here are a few more of my designs; I hope you'll find one that's just right for you. The full-size plans for these boats are available from Chesapeake Light Craft, Inc. (see Appendix C for the address and phone number).

Cape Charles 17

LOA: 17 feet
Beam: 24 inches
Weight: 37 pounds

This is a smaller version of the Cape Charles kayak described in this book. It is best suited to those who paddle with a total loaded weight (including paddler) of 130 to 250 pounds. If you weigh less than 190 pounds and don't plan long camping trips, I strongly urge you to build this boat instead of the 18-foot version.

Cape Charles 15.5

LOA: 15½ feet
Beam: 23 inches
Weight 34 pounds

Here is a still smaller Cape Charles. This one is for paddlers who weigh 90 to 140 pounds or who never plan to carry a total load of more than 190 pounds.

Cape Charles 13.5

LOA: 13½ feet
Beam: 22 inches
Weight: 30 pounds

The sleek and speedy Patuxent 17.5 has a slightly upswept bow.

This is a Cape Charles for kids. It's built exactly like the original and it's awfully cute.

Patuxent 17.5

LOA: 17½ feet
Beam: 22 inches
Weight: 36 pounds

This narrow hard-chine kayak is built much like the Cape Charles but is faster, lower, tippier, and more fun to paddle. It's designed for the skilled paddler who wants a high-performance Greenland-style kayak but needs to be able to carry enough gear for a week-long trip. I consider this my best-looking design to date.

Severn

LOA: 14½ feet
Beam: 26 inches
Weight: 28 pounds

Pictured on page 21, this compounded plywood design is a stable day-touring kayak. Its efficient hull (low wetted surface area) shape allows weaker, or less skilled, paddlers to keep up at normal touring speeds. Though some builders do paddle their Severns on the ocean, it was designed as a flatwater boat.

The Tred Avon double is built just like a big Cape Charles.

Tred Avon

LOA: 21 feet
Beam: 29 inches
Weight: 60 pounds

The Tred Avon is a roomy coastal-touring double based on the Cape Charles design. It can be built out of four 4 × 8 sheets of 4mm plywood in either an open- or a two-cockpit configuration.

Index